To:

_____

From:

_____

Date:

_____

Grace for Today

© 2008 Christian Art Gifts, RSA
       Christian Art Gifts Inc., IL, USA

Second edition 2013

Designed by Christian Art Gifts

Images used under license from Shutterstock.com

Compiled by Kylie Munger from the following devotionals by Solly Ozrovech: *The Abundant Life, Face to Face, The Voice behind You* and *A Shelter from the Storm.*

Printed in China

ISBN 978-1-4321-0915-8

14 15 16 17 18 19 20 21 22 23 – 11 10 9 8 7 6 5 4 3 2

GRACE FOR
TODAY

christian
art gifts.

January

Celebrating Life

Live Life to the Full

For with You is the fountain of
life; in Your light we see light.

Psalm 36:9

Life is the best thing God has given to you. So
be grateful for it. When you accept the goodness of life, you will stop fighting against it.

When you accept that life is good, all impa-
tience and frustration will be removed and life
becomes a satisfying and exciting experience.

Allow your life to be controlled by godly
principles and it will become an expression of
those plans. You will possess a unity with the
Creator, and your life will be filled with the
fullness of God.

*Creator God, I thank You that You have a plan for my
life that is filled with the fullness of You. Amen.*

January 1

Where Are You Heading?

Thanks be to God, who always leads
us in triumphal procession in Christ.

2 Corinthians 2:14

It is not always easy to choose which road you should follow. But accepting Christ as Lord of your life puts divine powers into action. Your values in Him will provide you with an inspired yet practical goal.

Choosing your goal and objectives with Christ will put you on the right road and will bring joy, confidence and enthusiasm into your life.

If you walk through life in the light of God, the whole journey becomes a joyous experience.

Dear Guide, thank You that I can walk through
life with You and that You guide me
along the paths of life. Amen.

A New Year with God

"I will instruct you and teach you in the way you should go; I will counsel you and watch over you."

Psalm 32:8

The prospect of a new year can be exciting because of many new possibilities and opportunities, but also disquieting if you face the future with anxiety – wondering whether the problems and disasters of the past will repeat themselves.

International crises, financial setbacks, as well as personal problems and disappointments tend to cloud our vision of the future.

Always remember that you can place your hope in the omniscience of God. He truly cares about you and He loves you deeply. Believe in the promises of Jesus and approach the new year in His loving presence. He will guide you through the labyrinth of life because He knows what is best for you.

You are truly a God of love! Thank You for sending Your only Son so that I, too, can be saved. Amen.

Something to Live For

"Before long, the world will not see Me anymore, but you will see Me. Because I live, you also will live."

John 14:19

Many people harbor anxiety because the future is unknown to them, and become pessimistic and discouraged. We must constantly remind ourselves that life is extremely precious, so that we don't fall into the trap of depression.

Even if the future seems bleak, you can be assured that your life and future are in God's hands. God is in control of everything. There is joy in Christ because He is the Rock on which you can build your life. His grace is sufficient to get you through each day.

Seize this life and live it in the abundance of Jesus Christ your Lord and Savior.

Through all the changing circumstances of life, Lord, in joy as well as sorrow, my heart will sing Your praises and thank You for the abundant life that You have made possible for me. Amen.

An Open Door

> "See, I have placed before you an
> open door that no one can shut."
>
> Revelation 3:8

Constant grumbling and drudgery makes life seem meaningless. It doesn't take someone who lives like this long to wilt intellectually and to develop a negative, cynical attitude towards life.

But Christ wants so much more for us. Scripture, history and personal experience offer ample testimony to the fact that an ordinary, seemingly meaningless life can be transformed by the power of the living Christ and through His Holy Spirit.

This new life of abundance that Christ offers you is yours for the taking. Turn to Christ and He will open the door to a new, meaningful life for you.

Lord Jesus, the open door of Your grace leads me into
the abundance and joy of life in Your presence. Fill
my life with new purpose and meaning today. Amen.

Experience Christ's Fullness

God was pleased to have all His fullness dwell in Him,
and through Him to reconcile to Himself all things.

Colossians 1:19-20

Jesus was not just "a good person", He was more than good. He was the personification of perfection.

This breathtaking truth is so overwhelming that we might even hesitate to approach the Lord. But, if He is your Savior, there is no barrier that can separate you from Him. Because of this, life becomes filled with fullness!

Read Ephesians 3:17-18 again, "So that Christ may dwell in your hearts through faith. And I pray that you, being rooted and established in love, may have power, together with all the saints, to grasp how wide and long and high and deep is the love of Christ."

How privileged we are, as God's children, to partake in His festival of love.

I praise and glorify You, O Loving Savior, that,
through faith, You abide in my heart.
Make it a worthy abode. Amen.

January 6

Life in All Its Fullness

That you may be filled to the measure
of all the fullness of God.

Ephesians 3:19

There are people who have lost interest in life
and are filled with despair because of circumstances or negative dispositions.

Although setbacks, which shake the core of
our very foundations, and disappointments are
a part of life, we must never lose sight of Jesus.
He came so that we may have abundant life.
He promises to be with us in every situation;
He promises to carry our burdens. All we need
to do is turn to Him in faith.

Enter into an intimate relationship with the
living Christ through prayer and meditation.
Share your problems with Him, and you will
experience profound joy and peace.

*Lord, You sprinkle Your blessings over me like
soft rain. You gladden my heart. Grant me
the fullness of Your Spirit. Amen.*

January 7

Positive Thinking

*Be transformed by the renewing of your mind.
Then you will be able to test and approve what God's
will is – His good, pleasing and perfect will.*

Romans 12:2

The teachings of our Lord embraces positive thinking, but it reaches beyond thoughts to touch the hidden possibilities of the spirit.

When we face the reality of situations in our lives, positive thinking can help up to a point, but a relationship with the living Christ can do so much more.

Positive thinking can only bring about limited solutions. Real change comes when you move past thinking, to an unshakable trust of God's work in your life.

Positive thinking, together with solid faith in the Almighty Christ, is a creative force that enables you to live as God intended you to live – in victory and with joy.

Holy Spirit, fill my heart with courage and the faith to know the good, perfect and pleasing will of God. Amen.

The Future Is Yours

*"I have come that they may have
life, and have it to the full."*

John 10:10

Perhaps your past tells a story of frustration or you feel that your life is uninspired and dull, and that nothing you do is worthwhile.

But the future belongs to you; it is yours. Every day is a gift from the loving hand of God, and you can only live life to the full when you surrender to His purpose for your life.

Achieving your purpose in life depends on your relationship with Christ. If your life has a spiritual foundation, it must also have a spiritual goal. It is by acknowledging this truth and applying it in your own life that you are guaranteed complete deliverance, joy and fulfillment. Then you can utilize God's precious gift of living life to the full.

*Thank You that I can have everlasting life
through Christ's crucifixion. Not even
death can make me fear. Amen.*

Make Today Wonderful

This is the day the Lord has made;
let us rejoice and be glad in it.

Psalm 118:24

Regardless of how bad things appear, God is greater than any situation.

Every day is a unique gift to you from God. What you make of it is your responsibility. The way in which you welcome each new day will depend on your frame of mind and attitude towards life.

Fortunately, your frame of mind is not something that you have to leave in the hands of fate or coincidence. God has given you the ability to choose your frame of mind, as well as the pace of your life. Meet every day with joy and expectation, and then you can live a happy, victorious life!

Father, I experience the reality of Your presence every moment of the day. Teach me to number my days in such a way that I will become wise. Amen.

Appreciate Life

I will sacrifice a thank offering to You
and call on the name of the Lord.

Psalm 116:17

Do you appreciate the love and support of your family? Can you still marvel at the rising of the sun? Can you still laugh about a funny situation, or do you find it hard to believe that humor is one of God's gifts to you?

Don't let your enthusiasm for life wane! Enjoying and appreciating the beauty of life must be an integral part of your life.

If you put God at the center of your life and thoughts, you will discover that, by appreciating your life, you continually move closer to Him, the Source of all real life.

Father, I appreciate all the beauty and joy that fills my life and that You have so freely bestowed on me. Amen.

January 11

Be Transformed

For with You is the fountain of
life; in Your light we see light.

Psalm 36:9

The quality of your life depends on your attitude and the way in which you approach and plan your life.

In God's Word you will find numerous examples of people who had seemingly useless, unimportant lives, and yet they were transformed into inspired disciples through Jesus.

Christ specifically came that you may have life in abundance. Turn to Him and walk your life's path in the company of the living Christ; you will discover a new self-confidence and develop abilities that can only be received from the Holy Spirit.

Holy Spirit, I plead that You would help me to make decisions that lead to life and that bring joy. Amen.

Find Joy in the Small Things

Everything God created is good, and nothing is to be rejected if it is received with thanksgiving.

1 Timothy 4:4

Many of us tend to take things for granted – the colors of flowers, the songs of birds, the beauty of a sunrise – these are all things that many people barely notice.

It is only when you begin to contemplate a life without these blessings that you realize how colorless and uninteresting it would be if they were absent.

We should cherish and appreciate every blessing in our lives. We should learn to appreciate the wonders of God's Creation and everything He has granted us through His grace.

Heavenly Father, I thank You for the everyday things in my life and for what they mean to me. Amen.

Live Fully

> We pray this in order that you may live a life
> worthy of the Lord and may please Him in
> every way: bearing fruit in every good work,
> growing in the knowledge of God.
>
> Colossians 1:10

People often seem to be bored or dissatisfied with life. Every moment of Jesus' life on earth was filled with purpose and meaning, and in everything He did the will of the Father and brought glory and honor to His name.

God expects you to follow in Jesus' footsteps – right here and now. Enter into His holy presence often and allow Him to fill your life with new purpose, new goals and new joy.

Let your attitude be the same as Jesus'. Fulfill His will and obey Him in all things and your life will yield a rich harvest that will glorify God.

*Perfect Example and Redeemer, through You I can
rejoice in the blessed knowledge that I can experience
true life in all its richness and fullness. Amen.*

Reach Your Goals

Walk in His ways, and keep His decrees and
commands, His laws and requirements, so that
you may prosper in all you do.

1 Kings 2:3

Few people can honestly say that success means
nothing to them.

For those who have a passionate desire to
succeed, failure can be a bitter pill to swallow.
Many people lose confidence and even give up
because they fear that they will never obtain
success.

It is important to accept the fact that it is
impossible to be successful through your own
abilities. You need Jesus Christ's guidance and
support to help you make the right decisions.

If the living Christ is your partner in life,
then you can rest assured that everything you
do will bring a deep and lasting sense of fulfillment.

*Holy Spirit, please help me to stay on course
and to achieve success in all that You
have called me to do. Amen.*

Life Is an Open Door

*"See, I have placed before you an
open door that no one can shut."*

Revelation 3:8

For some people, life is one uninteresting day after another in a meaningless existence.

But it doesn't have to be this way! Jesus has given you the promise of an abundant life. An ordinary, dull life can be transformed by the power of the living Christ through His Holy Spirit. Through the wonder of God's grace, sadness turns into joy, defeat into victory, fear disappears, hate changes to love, and despair to hope.

The moment you accept Christ into your life as Redeemer and Savior, you enter the door of redemption into a new world of vibrant, abundant life.

*Lord Jesus, the open door of Your grace leads me into
a life full of hope and happiness. Thank You for
putting purpose in my days. Amen.*

God Makes Life Good

"Listen to this, Job; stop and consider God's wonders."

Job 37:14

We live in troubled and uncertain times where basic values and integrity have been pushed aside. Sadly, many people have given up trying to promote a sense of morality and have chosen to just go with the flow.

If you are in this position, then, like Job, you should pause and consider God's wonders.

Reflect on the wonderful deeds of God. Out of chaos and darkness He created this beautiful earth. He loved us so much that He saved us from the bonds of sin and death. Through the life of Jesus He gave us an example of the fullness of life.

Praise Him for all His wonderful deeds and for His indescribable grace.

Lord, You fill my heart with gladness. Thank You for Your glorious deeds I see all around me every day. Amen.

January 17

Remember Who You Are

So God created man in His own image,
in the image of God He created him.

Genesis 1:27

When it seems as if nothing in your life is working out, when loneliness takes hold of you and despondency descends upon you, it is time to remember a few spiritual facts.

You were created in the very image of God. You are a spiritual being with a rich spiritual heritage.

You do not need to be at the mercy of moods and emotions beyond your control. You have been created for spiritual greatness, and when you live in the awareness of God's presence, you will be fulfilled.

*My Savior, because of my spiritual heritage and
the awareness of Your living presence, I can
face life with confidence. Amen.*

Be Enthusiastic

I will sacrifice a thank offering to You
and call on the name of the LORD.

Psalm 116:17

To really appreciate life, you need to keep your enthusiasm constantly alive. The gift of life must never be taken for granted or it becomes common and boring and you lose your sense of anticipation and vision for the future. Take time to enjoy and appreciate the beauty of life.

What are you taking for granted? Your daily existence can so easily degenerate into mindless drudgery. If you practice the art of appreciation, however, you can change your life into a beautiful and exciting adventure.

Father, I appreciate all the beauty and wonder that fills my life day by day. Through praise, You keep my heart sensitive to the needs of others. Amen.

Count Your Blessings

Whoever invokes a blessing in the land will
do so by the God of truth.

Isaiah 65:16

To the optimist, the simple things in life are a constant source of joy – spontaneous laughter, the bright rays of the sun, and the sounds of the birds in the trees.

People who count their blessings are extremely happy. Even in their darkest moments they maintain a spirit of hope and optimism, because they know things will work out well.

The more you count your blessings, the more it will seem as if God pours them out upon your life. Your heart will overflow with gratitude for God's amazing love. When life becomes a burden and it seems ominously dark around you, recalling your blessings is a sure way to keep a healthy perspective.

Father, how will I ever be able to express my gratitude in words? You bless me with so many things that were I to start listing them one by one, I would need eternity to thank You. Amen.

January 20

Spontaneous Thanksgiving

Your ways, O God, are holy. What god is so great as our God? You are the God who performs miracles; You display Your power among the peoples.

Psalm 77:13-14

We serve a wonderful God and King! Unfortunately we sometimes lose sight of His greatness and end up leading petty, unfulfilled lives. Instead of growing into the fullness of His stature by focusing on Him, we try to reduce Him to our level.

God is great and Scripture resounds with His invitation for us to share in His greatness. Surrendering to His presence transforms dwarves into spiritual giants.

When you are aware of God living in you, your attitude to life changes and your heart will overflow with gratitude for the glory and beauty that God imparts to your daily life.

Wondrous God, because You dwell in me through Jesus Christ I can overcome all the negative things in life and be filled with all the goodness of Your Holy Spirit. Amen.

A Reason to Live

"Because I live, you also will live."

John 14:19

Despite how gloomy the future seems sometimes, it is important to remember that your life and future are in the hands of God. The Christian's fate is not ruled by blind fate; God is in control of every situation in which you find yourself. He knows your needs and is always able to provide for you.

Through His death and resurrection Jesus not only gave you life, but also a reason to live. Through His Holy Spirit He provides you with the skills to cope with life. Choose life and live it in the abundance of Jesus Christ, giving Him the glory.

Faithful Lord, in the midst of change and corruption that occurs daily, I know that Jesus lives and that He has made it worthwhile for me to be alive too. Amen.

Days When
Things Go Wrong

"To whom do you belong, and where are you going, and
who owns all these animals in front of you?"

Genesis 32:17

Life must have purpose and significance if you
are to live meaningfully. One of the great truths
of the Christian life is that it changes your attitude. Previously you lived without hope or
expectation, but Christ now plants new hope
in your heart.

When you truly start living in Christ, you
look at life with new understanding. You will
never again have to ask, "Is life worthwhile?"
When the thoughts of Christ fill you and the
Holy Spirit saturates your spirit, you realize the
rich quality of your faith, and your life takes on
new and exciting dimensions.

*Lord Jesus, You came so that we may have abundant
life. Help me to remember to come to You when
days are dark, so that my life may be infused with
significance and meaning once again. Amen.*

Your Words
Are My Delight

When Your words came, I ate them; they were my joy and my heart's delight. Therefore this is what the Lord says: "If you repent, I will restore you that you may serve Me; if you utter worthy, not worthless, words, you will be My spokesman."

Jeremiah 15:16, 19

In answer to his prayer, God told Jeremiah that he should speak words that have value. Words can be used for either positive or negative means. Think carefully about how your words can be used for good rather than evil. The prophet Jeremiah said to the Lord, "Your words were my joy and my heart's delight."

God's encouraging words helped him and supported him greatly during the persecution that he had to endure. God wants to help you too. Let your words before God always be positive and let His Word always be a joy in your prayer life.

Lord God, help me to always speak words that are worthy and that bring glory and honor to You. Amen.

A New Year; a New Way; the Same God!

I will instruct you and teach you in the way you
should go; I will counsel you and watch over you.

Psalm 32:8

When we reflect on the future, we often allow
the events of the past – problems and disappointments – to cloud our vision.

Today, more so than ever before, the moment has come to place your unwavering trust
in the omniscience of God. He truly cares about
you and loves you deeply.

Everyone has a need for love: true, profound,
sincere love. So rediscover that, in this seemingly loveless world, there is Somebody who
has a special interest in you: a God in heaven
who is Love and who loves you dearly.

*You are truly a God of love! Thank You for sending
Your only Son to bring about my salvation too. Amen.*

Seize the Day!

*"In the time of My favor I heard you, and
in the day of salvation I helped you."*

2 Corinthians 6:2

When you look back on your life, there are certain highlights that tend to stand out – great moments in your life.

The truth is that every day could be a great day in your life if only you appreciated the present and passing moment. Every day is a new birth, with new prospects and opportunities that fall to you from the loving hand of God, so that you can live.

Cherish your memories, but appreciate the importance and wonderful possibilities of today. Accept every moment of every day as a gift of grace from the hand of God and utilize it fully. Then every day will be a great day.

*When I am confused and surrounded by darkness,
I know that You will deliver me. You are great and
good and do not scorn my feeble prayers. Thank
You for Your constant presence. Amen.*

The Road Ahead

"Have I not commanded you? Be strong
and courageous. Do not be terrified; do not
be discouraged, for the LORD your God
will be with you wherever you go."

Joshua 1:9

Many people try to discover the secrets of what
the future holds, but nobody really knows what's
in store for us.

Instead of fretting about the unknown, prepare yourself for any eventuality that God may
bring on your path. To be able to enter the unknown future in hope and trust, a positive and
living faith in God is imperative.

When Christ lives in your heart and in your
thoughts, you will be able to face the future
without fear. You will have the quiet assurance
that you will not be confronted by any situation that you and the living Christ will not be
able to overcome together.

*Lord, I rejoice in the knowledge that You hold my life
in Your hands. I trust You with my entire life. Amen.*

A Life of Happiness

I know that there is nothing better for men than to be happy and do good while they live.

Ecclesiastes 3:12

It is not a sin to be happy. Your heavenly Father gave you a life to be treasured and enjoyed to the full. If it is filled with the spice of laughter and humor, you are that much richer.

Live your life so that it is interspersed with joy and happiness. You have reason for great joy: God loves you, Christ died for you and the Holy Spirit leads you onto joyous paths.

The sublime peace of God is the main source of all true happiness. Make time to live life to the full, and with the help of the Holy Spirit develop a cheerful and positive outlook on life.

Lord, You are present in every phase of my life.
You comfort me in sorrow, but You also bless
me in abundance. With You by my side, I
will not be afraid of anything. Amen.

January 28

Say "Yes" to Life

> "I have come that they may have life,
> and have it to the full."
>
> John 10:10

The year ahead is a time of boundless opportunity to do good and to grow spiritually and intellectually. Remember, the future belongs to you and you can do with it whatever you want to because God has given you freedom of choice.

God, in His grace, gave you life with a sublime purpose. Every day is a gift from the loving hand of God, but you can only live life to the full when you subject yourself to His purpose for your life.

The abundant life belongs to God and, even though He is generous with this gift, He can only give it to those who are willing to receive and use it. So, say "yes" to life: it is your privilege as well as your responsibility.

Thank You that I may have everlasting life
through Christ's crucifixion. Not even
death can make me tremble. Amen.

Assess Yourself

Do not think of yourself more highly than you ought.

Romans 12:3

Many people have a poor opinion of themselves and their abilities. Such people lead unhappy and frustrated lives, because that which you believe of yourself is inevitably reflected in your way of life.

As a Christian disciple, sooner or later you must assess yourself in the light of God's Holy Spirit. This could be a humbling experience or it could reveal a revelation, and you will begin to see who you can become through God's strength, wisdom and inspiration.

Stop disparaging yourself and convincing yourself that you will never achieve anything worthwhile. You were created in the image of God and in His eyes you are invaluable. If you embrace this truth, the honest assessment of your life is about to begin.

Jesus Christ, I am endlessly grateful to have been redeemed by Your blood. Through You I can inherit eternal life. Amen.

January 30

Lean on God

From the fullness of His grace we have
all received one blessing after another.

John 1:16

Sometimes life and circumstances can get you
down. If you are feeling depressed or pessimistic, it is up to you to refresh your spirit by en-
tering into an intimate relationship with the
living Christ through prayer and meditation.

Like a needy child, tell God about all your
problems and concerns. Share your troubles
and anxieties with Him. The Word says, "Cast
all your anxiety on Him because He cares for
you" (1 Pet. 5:7). Do this and you will experience joy and peace like only God can give.

Through God's immense grace you will find
meaning and direction for your life, and your
life will be crowned with the success of God.

Lord, thank You that because of Your unfailing love,
I have a reason to celebrate life no matter what
trials I'm going through. Amen.

January 31

February

Keeping the Faith

The Lord Is Our Shepherd

The LORD is my shepherd, I shall not be in want.

Psalm 23:1

Those of us who belong to the Lord know we are safe and secure. We know for certain that the Lord is our Shepherd and therefore we do not fear the future because our Shepherd is already there. He will walk before us every day, leading us to our eternal destination.

Sometimes we have doubts about the future. We wonder whether we will have enough to provide for our essential needs. With childlike certainty, the psalmist then tells us, "I shall not be in want." You shall not be "in want" of anything that you truly need and that is good for you. The Lord will hear when you call, because His love never changes.

Lord God, it is a glorious reassurance to me that You are my Shepherd and that in Your hands I am safe and secure. Amen.

Spiritual Maturity

You, however, are controlled not by the sinful nature but
by the Spirit, if the Spirit of God lives in you.

Romans 8:9

The direction that your life has taken reveals
where the emphasis in your life lies. You may
achieve your material objectives, but is that
enough? Is that why God gave you life?

Remember, you are also a spiritual being,
therefore, your spirit can only ever be fully sat-
isfied when it is in a dynamic relationship with
the Holy Spirit.

This intimately personal relationship with
God can only be attained by faith in the resurrected Christ; a faith that is more than a fleeting emotion; a faith that accepts His authority
in all aspects of life. This type of faith will give
true sense and meaning to your life.

*I never want to be separated from You, Lord. I wish
to experience Your love and be a fruitful vine in
Your kingdom. I want to glorify You. Amen.*

February 2

When Dark Clouds Gather

Surely God is my salvation; I will trust and not be afraid. The LORD, the LORD, is my strength and my song; He has become my salvation.

Isaiah 12:2

It is a fact of life that sometimes storm clouds gather, darkening our lives, and it is futile to ignore them, hoping they will disappear.

Instead, stand firm with a living faith in the Almighty God, who controls the storms and hurricanes.

However threatening the circumstances of life may be, it is imperative that you do not allow anything to take God's central role in your life. With Him as the center you will maintain your balance. The ominous clouds might still be present, but you will be assured that your loving Father is working everything together for your good.

Even when everything around me is shrouded in darkness, You will shield me. Thank You, Father. Amen.

Get the Most
from Your Faith

"Whoever has will be given more, whoever does not
have, even what he has will be taken from him."

Matthew 13:12

Unfortunately, some people have never been inspired to walk intimately with the Lord. As a result of this, their faith is weak and their discipleship is ineffectual.

The world needs disciplined Christians to affirm and proclaim the teachings of Jesus, particu-
larly His command, "As I have loved you, so you
must love one another" (John 13:34).

The discipline that is needed to live a life of
Christian love demands a strength that can only
come from the Holy Spirit. This is nurtured
through prayer, Bible study and a hunger for a
more profound experience with God.

*I plead with You, O Jesus, for the gift of Your Holy
Spirit so that my faith can be fully experienced. Amen.*

Faith Is a Process of Growth

Grow in the grace and knowledge of our
Lord and Savior Jesus Christ.

2 Peter 3:18

It is sad that many Christians make little progress in their spiritual lives after accepting Christ as their Savior.

Ask yourself: Is Christ becoming more real to me? Is prayer essential in my decision-making? Do I find God's will for my life in the Scriptures? Am I nearer to Christ than I was when I was born again?

It takes courage to answer these questions. Allow this to be a prelude to renewing your faith in Christ and there will be no end to the growth and development it will bring forth. This growth will bring life-giving energy, enabling you to develop in Christlikeness and bear fruit in God's kingdom.

You are the true Vine, Lord. Keep me from evil and
help me to be truly fruitful in You. Amen.

A Most Enriching Experience

"Remain in Me, and I will remain in you."

John 15:4

It is worth remembering that the stars are still shining, even when clouds hide them. Remember, too, that behind the dark patches of life, the eternal love of your heavenly Father is still shining brightly. If you have cultivated trust in Him, your faith will carry you through the darkest moments of life.

The life that Jesus promises us if we "remain in Him" is such a challenge that people hesitate to accept it and instead choose to remain in a religious rut that promotes neither joy nor spiritual growth.

The life that Christ promises is much more than an emotional experience. It creates inner peace, a constructive purpose in life, and provides the strength to achieve and maintain such a life through the power of the Holy Spirit.

Holy Father, I praise and glorify You for the life-changing strength that flows from Christ. Amen.

God Is in Control

Job replied to the Lord: "I know that You can do all
things; no plan of Yours can be thwarted."

Job 42:1

Everywhere you go you will meet pessimistic
people – people who see no hope for the future and carry an atmosphere of gloom around
with them.

Rather than give in to despair, consider the
greatness of God. Look back over the years and
you will find many examples of the wonderful ways in which God transforms despair into
hope; sorrow into joy; and defeat into victory.

When things around you appear dark and ter-
rifying, hold onto the promises of God. Remember the mighty deeds that He has performed,
and continue in confidence and with the certain
knowledge that He is wholly in control.

*Almighty God and loving Father, my heart's knowledge
that You are in control allows me to be courageous
even in dark days. Guide me on Your path
and keep my faith strong. Amen.*

Grow in Faith

Immediately the boy's father exclaimed, "I do believe; help me overcome my unbelief!"

Mark 9:24

Many Christians urge fellow believers to, "Just believe!" but it's not always as easy as that, especially when the storm clouds close in around you.

Fortunately, through the grace of God it is easy to develop a mature and sincere faith. Recall an incident in your life when something out of the ordinary happened and thank God for it. It might not be something big or significant, but when you recall the incident, it strengthens your faith in a wonderful way.

Make a habit of remembering small answers to prayer, and your faith will gradually grow to the extent where you will receive bigger revelations from God.

Loving Master, I want to grow in my faith so that I can bring glory and honor to You in everything I do and say. Amen.

Believing without Seeing

Therefore we are always confident.
We live by faith, not by sight.

2 Corinthians 5:6-7

When you are facing problems, difficulties or tough decisions, do you trust God sufficiently to put yourself and your future in His hands?

Jesus came to confirm that God loves you unconditionally. His care, help and compassion are unquestionable. You are precious in His sight. Therefore, Christ will not allow anything to harm you.

With this assurance, you can trust God unconditionally in everything. Then you will walk along His path, doing His will.

If you do this, you will experience peace and tranquility of mind. Even if you cannot see the complete road ahead, faith will carry you through.

Lord, please be with me in the dark days, and
shine the light of Your presence before
me so that I do not stumble. Amen.

Trust in God

As for me, I watch in hope for the LORD, I wait
for God my Savior; my God will hear me.

Micah 7:7

Some people look at the stars or consult for-
tune-tellers in order to "see" their future.

However trustworthy these methods seem,
they cannot help us handle the unknown. The
only way in which we can be filled with confidence about the future is by believing in God.

When you are facing a problem and doubt
tries to take hold of you, this is when Jesus comes
to you, saying, "Take courage! It is I. Don't be
afraid" (Matt. 14:27). Christ Himself will bring
you peace of mind.

*Loving Savior, I place myself completely under
Your control, for I know that You alone can
guarantee me peace of mind. Amen.*

Do You Truly Believe?

"I do believe; help me overcome my unbelief!"

Mark 9:24

How solid is your faith? Have you reduced it to outward matters of attending church, singing songs of praise, listening to nice sermons and trying to live a respectable life?

Your faith only becomes reality when the external ceremonies of Christianity become a pulsating and powerful experience in your soul. It becomes a reality when you no longer see yourself as someone defeated by sin because God's Holy Spirit, who resides in you, enables you to triumph over all sin.

You must develop the discipline of experiencing Christ's presence in your everyday life. Prayer, Bible study and fellowship with other believers are essential to attaining a positive, living and dynamic faith.

Lord, You are my only shelter. When I feel powerless and afraid, You will lead me through the darkness and give me renewed courage. Amen.

February 11

The Light on Your Way

God said, "Let there be light," and there was light.

Genesis 1:3

When we look back along the road we have traveled, we tend to focus only on the negative things. Because the past had its share of problems, many people expect the same from the future.

But this is a negative way of looking at life. The prayer of your heart every day should be, "Lead me, O Light of the world!" Jesus Christ is still the Light of the world and He has promised that those who follow Him will never walk in darkness. Take His hand in faith and trust and experience Him as the light of your life.

God of light and truth, thank You that Your Son has illuminated my life so that I can walk into the future in faith and trust. Be my light, even when darkness falls around me. Amen.

God Remains in Control

He is before all things, and in Him
all things hold together.

Colossians 1:17

There are times when it seems as if everything is going wrong. Throughout history, nations and individuals have struggled through disasters, hardships, dangers, sorrow and adversity.

Before becoming despondent, however, acknowledge the greatness, glory and constancy of God. He called the world into existence, He created man and has kept vigil over His creation, caring for us through the ages and sheltering us in every disaster.

He is the Creator God who will never abandon His workmanship. Hold onto His promises; place your entire trust and faith in the living Christ and through Him you will survive all dangers and adversities.

You are eternal, Lord, and the workmanship of Your Creation bears testimony to Your great glory. Amen.

Blessed Assurance

Commit to the Lord whatever you do,
and your plans will succeed.

Proverbs 16:3

Planning is important in every area of life. You plan for the future, for your marriage, for your finances and for retirement. Much of our time and energy goes into planning.

There is a way to make planning better, however, but it requires strict spiritual discipline to make it effective and it must be undertaken with sincerity and honesty. It also requires solid faith and trust in God and in His promises.

Whatever your concern may be, lay it before God in prayer with all your fears and expectations, trusting Him completely.

Leave the matter in God's hands. In His own perfect time and way, He will show you how to bring it to pass.

*Dear Lord, guide me to follow Your commands
and to fulfill Your will in obedience. Amen.*

Faith That Counts

The only thing that counts is faith
expressing itself through love.

Galatians 5:6

People have different opinions regarding what
is most important in our spiritual lives.

Your faith will be insufficient and ineffective if it does not lead you to a more profound
knowledge and awareness of God.

Faith is alive and meaningful when it is ex-
pressed through love. Without love, faith becomes dead and the height, depth and eternal
nature of God's love cannot be experienced. If
you posses a living faith, manifested in love,
you have the basic qualities of a practical, inspired and effective religion that is acceptable
to God.

Lord, Your Word teaches me to love You with my
whole heart, soul and mind, and to love my neighbor
as myself. Grant me the strength to abide by
these commandments. Amen.

God Has a Plan for You

Do not be distressed and do not be angry with yourselves for selling me here, because it was to save lives that God sent me ahead of you.

Genesis 45:5

It is often difficult to understand that God is fulfilling His plan in your life, especially when times are tough. When Joseph was sold into slavery, he probably struggled to discern God's will. Nevertheless, many years later, he recognized that God had been with him through it all.

God determines the pattern of your life. In your present circumstances, difficult as they might be, hold on to the assurance that God is busy working out His perfect plan for your life. Life's darkest moments can become a testimony of God's perfect purpose for your life.

Faithful Guide, I will trust You to lead me surely along the pathways through life, even when the dark shadows hide my way. Amen.

February 16

Conquer Depression

"For you who revere My name, the sun of righteousness
will rise with healing in its wings."

Malachi 4:2

Depression and pessimism are ailments that can
destroy a person's soul. Apart from the fact that
depression is an illness of the mind, it also affects
your physical and spiritual well-being, limits
your vision of the future, and negatively influences your attitude towards life.

The only way to fight such an emotional disruption effectively is to turn to Christ and open
yourself to His love and healing.

Place yourself unconditionally in His care.
When Jesus guides you along the path you need
to take through life, you will find that because of
your obedience to Him, you will be filled with
a sense of self-confidence and well-being that
only He can give you.

*I cling to You, Lord Jesus, in the knowledge
that nothing in this life can harm me as
long as You are with me. Amen.*

Comfort in the Word

Open my eyes that I may see
wonderful things in Your law.

Psalm 119:18

Disillusionment and dejection are common among people who have developed a negative outlook on life.

In order to live and not merely exist, it is essential to nurture a positive attitude – even when things are not going well. Your faith will need to be strong if you are to triumph over your problems with joy.

Scripture is filled with stories of how ordinary people, like you and me, overcame hostile forces in the name of the Lord. Draw comfort from the Word and through Jesus Christ, the incarnate Word. Then you will be able to triumph over any adversity.

You reveal Yourself in Your Word. It is trustworthy, steadfast and unfailing. Thank You that I can know the abundant life that is found in Your Word. Amen.

God's Love Endures Forever

Though I walk in the midst of trouble, You preserve
my life. The LORD will fulfill His purpose for me;
Your love, O LORD, endures forever – do not
abandon the works of Your hands.

Psalm 138:7-8

You might sometimes feel that God has abandoned you when you needed Him most. But
through faith you need to hold fast to what you
know is true about God, even when you cannot
see any results.

Although we are inclined to plan our whole
course through life, we can confess, together
with David, "The LORD will fulfill His purpose
for me." In the time of his worst trial, David still
trusted God to protect him. Be assured that the
Lord will never neglect the work of His hands,
so even in the dark times, remember that God
is faithful and you can never drift too far away
from the sphere of His love.

Loving God, protect me from the anger of my enemies.
Thank You that there is no end to Your love. Amen.

Find Strength in God

O Lord, be gracious to us; we long for You. Be our strength every morning, our salvation in time of distress.

Isaiah 33:2

Immediately after praying to God to save Israel, Isaiah describes Israel's distress: the Asyrians rejected their petition for peace, Lebanon was destroyed, and the plains of Sharon resembled a wilderness.

Isaiah's trust in God never faltered. He believed God's promises that He would preserve Israel and deliver His people. Because of this Isaiah could pray with confidence, "Be our strength every morning, our salvation in times of distress."

Like Isaiah, we can depend on God in times of distress and trouble. Call on Him in such times and feel the strength, that can only come from God, descend on you.

Omnipotent and omniscient God, help me to trust in Your promises. Be my strength and my salvation each day. Amen.

Living a "Faith Life"

"Lord, I believe; help my unbelief!"

Mark 9:24 (NKJV)

Is faith a living reality in your life? Faith only becomes real when you feel that you are triumphant and completely in control of your own life through God's Holy Spirit, which resides in you and enables you to conquer all circumstances.

It is true that salvation is God's liberating deed of grace towards mankind. However, it does not release you from the responsibility to accept Him with both your spirit and your intellect.

In order to live a "faith life" you must pursue the presence of God so that you may cultivate a living, bold faith.

Lord, help me to develop my faith so that in all circumstances, I choose to follow Your ways. Amen.

Faith Is a Process of Growth

Grow in the grace and knowledge of our Lord
and Savior Jesus Christ.

2 Peter 3:18

Christian life is all but static. While the revelation of God through Jesus Christ was a unique miracle, man's reaction to this manifestation of God's love is not something that just happens in a person's life only to be forgotten in the long run.

Despite past failures, the whisperings of the Holy Spirit will inspire you to develop an awareness of Christ's indwelling presence. There is no end to this kind of growth and development because the more you become aware of Christ's presence, the greater your love for Him becomes. This growth is the life-giving energy of your Christlikeness, enabling you to reach the fruit-bearing maturity in His kingdom.

Lord, thank You that if I pursue You and all Your
ways, I will be rewarded and bear fruit. Amen.

February 22

Let Jesus Guide You

Therefore we are always confident and know that as long as we are at home in the body we are away from the Lord. We live by faith, not by sight.

2 Corinthians 5:6-7

How often have you experienced doubt, loneliness and anxiety? When an important decision has to be made do you find it difficult to make the right choice? If so, you are relying on your own limited insight.

Regardless of the circumstances, put your plans, your doubts, your fears and your problems before the Lord's throne of grace and ask Jesus to be your Guide. Be sensitive to the whisperings and stirrings of the Holy Spirit in your life, and face the future with faith and hope. You can rest assured that the living Christ will be by your side, leading and guiding you.

Lord, let Your kindly light guide me. Help me to understand that I should take life one day at a time and seek Your guidance in everything I do. Amen.

Find Your Strength in God

Be strong in the Lord and in His mighty power.

Ephesians 6:10

In order to avoid feeling overwhelmed with anxiety and fear, uncertainty and inadequacy, it is essential to cling to Christ and draw your strength from Him. No one else but God knows you and your problems so intimately and completely, God loves you so much that He keeps a vigil of all-embracing love over you.

Armed with the assurance that you are supported and protected by the power, omnipotence, love and mercy of God, you should be equipped to deal with any situation that life might hand you.

Thank You for providing me with armor and shielding me against the shrewdness of Satan. You are my power and my strength. In You, Lord, I trust. Amen.

Productive Faith

He touched their eyes and said, "According
to your faith will it be done to you."

Matthew 9:29

There are people who regard faith as a mere commodity, something that you have a lot or very little of, depending on the circumstances.

You should, however, understand the importance and necessity of maintaining a disposition of expectation towards life. Only those who have an unfailing faith and trust in the Eternal God can face the future with courage and serenity. This great truth, and the acceptance of it in your life creates stability and enables you to face the future with confidence.

Help me Lord, to be steadfast in my faith and to be
forever devoted to Your work. Bless me in abundance
and help me to use it to Your greater glory. Amen.

Allow Faith to Dispel Fear

He said to His disciples, "Why are you so afraid?
Do you still have no faith?"

Mark 4:40

There are few people who do not harbor fear in one form or another. It is a strange fact that many people cannot explain the fear that haunts them but it is nevertheless a burning presence in their lives.

There is only one sure cure for a life that is dominated by fear, and that is a living faith in Jesus Christ. Fear and faith cannot co-exist in the same life. Faith nurtures faith and fear nurtures fear. Place your trust in God.

At first, in the little things in your life, His love and wisdom will be revealed and confirmed, and in time, the bigger things in your life will be under His control too.

As Your child, I know where to find veritable peace.
Dispel fear and selfishness from my heart, so
that I may serve You faithfully. Amen.

February 26

Confront Your Weaknesses

David found strength in the LORD his God.

1 Samuel 30:6

There are few people who can honestly say that they are equipped to meet and handle any situation with ease and confidence.

Regardless of what problems you face or how inadequate you might feel in any given situation – be it in the business world, on the home front, on the sports field, or even on a social level – you must surrender it in prayer to God. Ask Him to give you strength to handle the situation. Once you accept this and believe that He can and will do it, you can move forward with confidence in the knowledge that God's grace is sufficient to enable you to overcome your weaknesses.

Lord, even when I am filled with doubt; You are by my side. You give me strength to overcome daily temptation, so that one day I may behold Your splendor. Amen.

A Faith That Counts

The only thing that counts is faith
expressing itself through love.

Galatians 5:6

In order to be effective and powerful, faith must be nurtured. You must have an intimate relationship with Jesus Christ and love Him with such sincerity that His presence becomes a living reality in your life.

Set aside precious moments to be with Him. When you possess a living faith that manifests itself in love, you have the basic qualities of a practical, inspired and effective religion that is acceptable to God. Then it is a source of blessing, not only for you, but also for your fellow man.

Lord, Your Word teaches me to love You with my whole heart, soul and mind, and to love my neighbor as myself. Grant me the strength to abide by these commandments. Amen.

Steadfast in Faith

"Now be strong," declares the Lord, "and work.
For I am with you," declares the Lord Almighty.

Haggai 2:4

In the initial exciting phase of a person's born-again life, the Lord's work is done with zeal and enthusiasm. We are filled with the joy of a new life in Christ and we wish to share our feelings and ecstasy with others.

Whatever happens, do not succumb to the temptation to give up your work for Christ. Seek advice, help and guidance at all times but never allow discouragement to paralyze you in your honest pursuit to serve the Lord. Take courage and be steadfast in faith – through the mercy of Jesus Christ you will achieve success.

Your Creation, Lord, will never perish; it is everlasting.
Grant me the strength and make me Your servant so
that I may share in the fulfillment of Your will. Amen.

March

The Essence of Love

All-Surrounding Love

The LORD is my shepherd, I shall not want.

Psalm 23:1 (NKJV)

Sheep and goats were very precious to the Palestinian shepherds. The shepherds took special care of them by leading them to pastures and water, protecting them and searching for the ones that went astray.

Jesus calls Himself the Good Shepherd who cares for God's precious children. He provides for your daily needs, protects you, shows you the path of righteousness, and searches for you when you go off course. Then He lovingly brings you back to the safety of the flock.

The Good Shepherd offers us His protection and immeasurable love, and asks only that we love Him in return. Is this too high a price to pay for a love that exceeds all other loves?

Good Shepherd, thank You for Your special love and care that keeps and protects me day by day. Amen.

God's Redeeming Love

To them God has chosen to make known among the
Gentiles the glorious riches of this mystery, which is
Christ in you, the hope of glory.

Colossians 1:27

The wonder and glory of the Christian gospel
is that God loved us while we were still sinners.
Without such a love we would indeed have still
been lost.

As you become deeply aware of your imper-
fections and sin, you are also aware that there
is a divine and all-powerful Deity who is calling you to a better and nobler life. Because of
our sinfulness it is impossible to live life as God
intended for us without His help.

So accept God's offer to recreate and transform your life. Allow the Holy Spirit to fill you
with the strength you need to walk according
to God's ways.

*Lord, I am sincerely grateful that You bore my punish-
ment for sin and opened the way for me to come to
the Father and live according to His ways. Amen.*

True Love

Love must be sincere.

Romans 12:9

The word *love* is probably the most used and least understood word in any language.

Jesus Christ came to demonstrate the meaning of true love when He willingly gave His life for all humanity. He took our punishment upon Himself to redeem us from our sinfulness. As He said, "Greater love has no one than this, that he lay down his life for his friends" (John 15:13).

True love involves making sacrifices for the sake of another. It is tolerant, patient and understanding, even in the most trying circumstances. It involves forgiveness and giving of yourself for the benefit of others. It means to love others as Jesus loves you.

Loving Lord Jesus, help me to spread Your love in the world around me. Amen.

True Christianity

Examine yourselves to see whether
you are in the faith; test yourselves. Do
you not realize that Christ Jesus is in you?

2 Corinthians 13:5

Many people have the misconception that Christians are weak, dull, and ineffective; purposefully cutting themselves off from the rest of the world.

There was nothing weak, commonplace, or ineffective about Jesus Christ. The Scriptures bear witness to His humanity and His divinity; to His firmness and tenderness; to His courage and humility; and above all, to His love – even when He was subjected to bitter hatred, barbaric torture and death.

This is the example that our Leader set for all Christians to follow. Allow Him to transform you into a strong and effective witness of the powerful truth of the gospel of Christ.

*Thank You heavenly Father, that we are more
than conquerors through Your Son and
through Your Holy Spirit. Amen.*

Jesus Understands
Because He Loves You

Jesus wept. Then the Jews said,
"See how He loved him!"

Some people see Jesus as someone who is distant, and far removed from everyday life; concerned only with matters of universal importance, and not the inconsequential details of our personal lives.

This is not true. He has a loving interest in the world He created, as well as in the people for whom His Son died and was resurrected.

Never lose sight of the fact that Jesus is not only your Master, He is also your friend. Because He lived, suffered and died as a human being, He understands human problems and emotions. He endured suffering, as well as disappointment, sorrow and joy. The Son of God laughed and cried just as we do.

Lord Jesus, in You I have found a Friend who is always loving, faithful, and understanding. Amen.

The Holy Spirit – Cultivator of Love

God has poured out His love into our hearts by the Holy Spirit, whom He has given us.

Romans 5:5

The knowledge that Christ lives in you can inspire your thinking, deepen your insight, give you new confidence, create enthusiasm, and bring purpose and meaning to life.

If you love Christ, the Holy Spirit will begin to make you aware of the needs of others and you will be compelled to do something about them. Your words, your attitude, and your willingness to serve others in the power of the Spirit are the result of God's love in your heart.

God Himself is the source of this love, which Jesus Christ demonstrated to us, and the Holy Spirit cultivates in our hearts.

Holy Spirit, love Divine, glow within this heart of mine, kindle every high desire, perish self in Thy pure fire. Amen.

Spirit of Love

Hope does not disappoint us, because God has
poured out His love into our hearts by the Holy
Spirit, whom He has given us.

Romans 5:5

Jesus promised His Holy Spirit to everyone
who accepts Him as Lord and Savior and He
has kept this promise.

Remember that Christ can change your life.
As you open your heart to Him, a new unsur-
passed strength will fill your soul and enable
you to do those things that are pleasing to God.
This change and new strength are the work of
the Spirit and will assure you of Christ's presence in your life.

If you have the Spirit of Christ you will
know the reality of His holy presence. Love for
Him will radiate from your heart and life.

*I praise You, Lord, because I can experience the power
of Your living presence through the work of the Holy
Spirit and so I can love You with a pure heart. Amen.*

March 7

God's Great Gift

May the grace of the Lord Jesus Christ, and the
love of God, and the fellowship of the Holy
Spirit be with you all.

2 Corinthians 13:14

When we reflect on the sacrifice God made on
Golgotha, through Jesus Christ, for our redemption and salvation, the eternal hope that He
gave us through His triumphant resurrection
from the dead and the power He extends to us
through the Holy Spirit, we are overwhelmed
with wonder.

There is no way we could ever repay the
Lord for His immeasurable love. But we could,
and should, open our lives to Him so that we
can pass on His love to others. Christ commanded us to love one another as we love ourselves, and as He loves us.

Lord, I want to glorify You as my Father always.
Guide me, through Your Holy Spirit, so that I will
be obedient to You in everything I do. Amen.

The Extent of God's Love

"I have loved you," says the LORD. "But you ask, 'How have You loved us?'"

Malachi 1:2

In the midst of personal setbacks and tragedies, in hardships and disappointments, many people blame God for the situation they find themselves in and even turn their backs on Him because they judge God by human standards.

Tragically they do not see that the disasters of this world cannot be ascribed to a lack of love in the Father or the Son, but rather to the foolishness of man.

The love of God is revealed in His abundant blessing, His all-powerful forgiveness, His mercy, His promise of eternal life, His comfort, His gift of the Holy Spirit, and above all, the sacrifice of Jesus Christ on Golgotha. Do we need more proof than this?

Lord Jesus, I thank You for the privilege of knowing You. Thank You for taking me out of darkness and placing me in Your kingdom of light. Amen.

The Power of God's Love

> "You have let go of the commands of God and are
> holding on to the traditions of men."
>
> Mark 7:8

Rituals and traditions play an important role in society. While it is essential that any group of people must adhere to rules so that everything can run smoothly, it is of the utmost importance that these rules do not become the dominant factor in the Christian community.

The foundation of any congregation must be absolute surrender, devotion and obedience to God. Jesus Christ must be central in all things and His will must take precedence over the will of people.

To be a channel of the love of God, surrender yourself unconditionally to the guidance of the Holy Spirit, then you will be able to serve your community according to God's will, and in love.

*Holy Spirit, bring me to total surrender, devotion,
and obedience to the God of love. Amen.*

God's Love Has No Price

> Peter answered: "May your money perish with you, because you thought you could buy the gift of God with money!"
>
> Acts 8:20

Many people believe that money can buy them everything. While this may be true of material possessions, it cannot buy things like peace, joy and fullness of life. These qualities have no price tags. They are God's gifts of grace to us.

We enjoy everything that is good and worthwhile by the grace of God. We don't deserve these things, we cannot earn them and we are not worthy of them, but we receive them because of Christ's unfathomable love and grace towards us.

Never take the blessings that you receive from His hand for granted. Always remember that they are gifts of God's eternal goodness and a sign of His love towards you.

I want to thank You for the undeserved gifts
that You bestow so graciously on my life –
for love and peace and hope. Amen.

Incredible but True

Now these three remain: faith, hope and love. But the greatest of these is love.

1 Corinthians 13:13

In these troublesome times, when bitterness and prejudice abound, it is hard to remember that love triumphs. Thousands of years ago, Christ was unjustly tried and mocked by the Roman soldiers and cruelly nailed to a wooden cross.

Our awe of Christ on the cross lies in the fact that in the midst of public scorn, derision and unbearable pain, He prayed for those who crucified Him. His love surpassed all the powers of hatred.

When crime and violence make a mockery of all that Jesus Christ lived for and taught, then remember Golgotha and focus on God's love. You will find peace and calm that will make you aware of the immortality and invincibility of love.

God, I ask that love will be the motivating factor of my life, as it is for Yours. Amen.

March 12

Surrounded by God's Love

*"For them I sanctify Myself, that they too may
be truly sanctified."*

John 17:19

There are probably times in your life when your
Christian walk seems like a struggle and your
faith grows weak. When this happens, shift your
focus and look at your life from Christ's view-
point. His involvement in your life of faith is
more important than your own. He is the one
who called you.

This divine calling does not depend on your
shifting emotions. He will bind you to Him with
cords of love. When you become despondent,
remember that the loving Christ will never
change. You still belong to Him, He loves you
and He is still your Lord. Christ's love for you
doesn't change according to your emotions; it
is eternal and unfailing.

*I thank You, O Guide, that my changing emotions
need not dictate the course of my life. Thank You
that Your love for me is constant. Amen.*

The Extent of Christ's Love

Do you show contempt for the riches of His kindness,
tolerance and patience, not realizing that God's
kindness leads you towards repentance?

Romans 2:4

When you consider all the evil in the world,
you become aware of the full extent of God's
love. People ignore Him, they forget His grace,
they disobey Him, they rebel against Him, and
they blame Him when things go wrong.

No human being would have tolerated the
attitude that mankind displays toward God,
and still show the infinite love that God does
toward His people. Acknowledge His merciful
acceptance of you as His child. Surrender yourself unconditionally to His Son. Praise Him,
follow Him and live life to the full as He offers
it to you.

*God of love, thank You that Your love and grace en-
abled me to find You. I surrender myself in
renewed love to You. Amen.*

The Power of God's Love

> People will oppress each other – man against man,
> neighbor against neighbor. The young will rise up
> against the old, the base against the honorable.
>
> Isaiah 3:5

In today's world it seems as if chaos and anarchy rule in every corner. However, this doesn't mean we need to tolerate the situation. In Christ Jesus, God came to fight against evil. He did this with the only weapon effective enough to overcome the forces of darkness. And it is just as powerful today – godly love.

God continues to spread His love over His children and it is the Christian's privilege and duty to share this love with others.

There is no other way of stopping the tide of evil that is threatening society today than to try to become a channel of God's love.

Holy God, make me an ambassador of Your love,
sharing it with everyone I meet. Amen.

Sincere Love

Love must be sincere.

Romans 12:9

Although we may doubt the sincerity of people's love, we need never doubt the sincerity of God's love for us. Love compelled Him to come to this world in the person of Jesus Christ and suffer and die on our behalf.

It was love that gave Him the victory over death and made Him ascend to heaven where He intercedes for us. It was love that urged Him to forgive our sins and offer us the gift of His Holy Spirit.

This world will never know any love greater than that of Jesus Christ. He gave us the example of sincere love and urges us to love as He loved.

God of love, please help me to never lose sight of the greatness of Your love for me, no matter what happens in my life. Amen.

Love without Boundaries

> They crucified Him. Dividing up His clothes,
> they cast lots to see what each would get.
>
> Mark 15:24

Throughout the ages people have rejected, ignored, denied and betrayed Jesus. Yet despite this, in times of need they still call on Him and ask for His help.

The marvel of the Christian faith is that regardless of how you treat Christ, He still loves you. He lavishes His boundless love on you and meets your needs.

The crucifixion shows us that the love of Christ knows no boundaries. It is a love so sincere and pure that nothing can withstand it. Whether you deserve it or not – this is the love that God wants to give to you through Jesus Christ. How then can you withhold your love from Him?

Lord, I want to share in the glory of Your love.
Fill me with Your love so that I can truly
love You as You deserve. Amen.

Love Brings Life

We know that we have passed from death to life,
because we love our brothers.

1 John 3:14

Everything Jesus was, everything He taught, and everything He did, was a manifestation of God's love. The love of God enriches the lives of everyone who allows Him to pour it into their hearts.

It is possible to experience the love of God firsthand and to allow your life to become a channel of God's love. This is the wisest way we can choose to live. The opposite of love is hate. Hate follows the path of bitterness, dissension and torn apart relationships.

When the love of God is a powerful force in your life and His love reaches out to others through you, your own life is enriched in a way you never thought possible.

Lord God, through Your Holy Spirit please do the impossible and enrich my life through the wonders of Your love. Amen.

Receive God's Love

He predestined us to be adopted as His sons through Jesus Christ, in accordance with His pleasure and will.

Ephesians 1:5

If the name and character of Jesus had not been love, it would have been impossible for imperfect and sinful people to enter into a relationship with Him. But because He is love, He calls you to Him.

As you open up your life to His influence, the Holy Spirit will enable you to live as God intended: in His strength and in the awareness of His living presence.

When God's love fills your life, you will experience a feeling of unity with Him. This intimacy isn't something that you can earn through your own efforts; it is a gift from God. It becomes yours when you receive it in faith and with gratitude.

Eternal God, Your unfathomable love is beyond my understanding, yet You have given it to me as a precious gift of Your grace. Amen.

God's Unfailing Love

"Though the mountains be shaken and the hills be removed, yet My unfailing love for you will not be shaken nor My covenant of peace be removed."

Isaiah 54:10

Most of us have experienced firsthand how the radically changing circumstances of life often have a dramatic influence on us, and on those whom we love. One moment we experience joy, the next we are swept into the depths of despair.

Regardless of these unexpected and unplanned events in your life, you have the assurance of God's love for you. However despondent you may be, never lose sight of the fact that Jesus loves you with an unfailing, eternal and perfect love.

Turn to Him in times of affliction and you will enjoy the blessings of the Lord, as well as His love that drives out all fear.

Lord, I feel safe in the palm of Your hand.
Thank You for sheltering me when the
storms of life rage around me. Amen.

God Loves You

We know that in all things God works for the good of those who love Him, who have been called according to His purpose.

Romans 8:28

People often cannot understand why trials and setbacks happen to them. Yet one of the basic components of Christianity is steadfast faith in the love of God. This love has been proven beyond a doubt in the gift of His Son to a lost world. That is why in every situation of life, you can put your trust in the wisdom and goodness of a loving Father.

When you find yourself facing problems or setbacks, remember that your life is in God's mighty hands. Because of His great love for you, everything that happens to you has a purpose.

Jesus, in the darkest moments of my life, thank You that I can be assured of the goodness of Your love that lets nothing happen to me by chance. Amen.

Let Your Love Be Selfless

Let us not love with words or tongue but with actions and in truth.

1 John 3:18

True love is not easily fathomed. Yet, of all the human emotions it is the most profound. We tend to reduce love to mushy sentimentality, thus diminishing it as a dynamic force and making it powerless and ineffective.

The basis for true love is identification with the loved one. It is to experience his or her joys, sorrows, temptations and disappointments. True love involves sacrifice and sorrow. The true quality of love surpasses sympathy and sentimentality, and manifests itself in loyalty and faithfulness.

Love in action is more than simply doing good deeds, pure love is profound and unselfish and embraces the faithfulness and noble principles that enrich the heart and mind of a person. It is precious above all things.

Father, enable me to love without counting the cost. Amen.

Love Is Practical and Sincere

This is how God showed His love among us:
He sent His one and only Son into the world
that we might live through Him.

1 John 4:9

Jesus Christ was deeply practical. If you study His life you will note that, along with the profound spirituality of His ministry, He had a truly practical nature. When Jesus raised Jairus's daughter from the dead, He told her parents to give her something to eat.

True love and care requires more than mere words – it calls for action. It is to support someone in prayer, but also to do something practical to show your love; even if it is inconvenient.

By demonstrating your love for others in a practical way, you follow the example Jesus set for us. He is our example because His love exceeds all other love.

Holy Jesus, help me to love others with a love that is practical and sincere. Amen.

Love Is the
Most Excellent Way

Now I will show you the most excellent way.

1 Corinthians 12:31

Jesus was the embodiment of God's perfect love. He calls us to walk the path of this love. No compromise can be tolerated. If we wish to follow the most excellent way, we must follow the way of His love.

A response to the challenge of Christian love calls for deep devotion. Even when you have given everything, you still want to give more. It is then that you open your life to the influence of the Holy Spirit. That which you cannot achieve by your own effort and strength, God will achieve through you.

His Holy Spirit residing in us makes the impossible possible. Choose the best – choose to love!

Lord, reveal Your love in my life so that I may love my neighbor. Help me to aspire to this commandment of Yours. Amen.

True Love Allows Freedom

He came to that which was His own, but His own did
not receive Him.

John 1:11

If you love someone you allow him or her the
freedom that their spirit needs. It is only by
setting someone free that the bonds of mutual
love may be strengthened.

The principle of generous love forms the basis of the Christian gospel. God allows you the
freedom of choice to either believe in Him or
reject Him. Christ does not want to compel you
to love Him. He invited you by grace to accept
Him and to associate with Him through a new
relationship of love.

If you accept His love and make His way of
life your own, you will delightfully discover
that your imperfect love reacts to His divine
love. Such a love brings about freedom, joy and
peace in your life.

*Take away my weariness, Lord, and allow Your
strength to flow through me. Amen.*

Establish Healthy Relationships

Be kind and compassionate to one another, forgiving
each other, just as in Christ God forgave you.

Ephesians 4:32

In life it is important to protect yourself against
selfishness, foolish pride, unkind thoughts and
other negative traits.

If you harden yourself against calls for help
or pleas for forgiveness, you harden your spirit.

The way to overcome a heartless and indifferent attitude is to approach life with the attitude
of Jesus Christ. Do not condemn, instead have
understanding and sympathy toward others.

A compassionate attitude allows the Spirit
of God to work through you and bring you to
the realization that only by being a blessing to
your fellow man can you receive the love and
blessing of God.

*Sometimes we are so indifferent to the world
around us. Help us, Lord, to support
others in neighborly love. Amen.*

The Christian's Deepest Desire

I want to know Christ.

Philippians 3:10

To be a Christian means knowing Christ and loving Him dearly. Jesus often taught that it is difficult to live isolated from love.

Love, because of its intrinsic nature, rises above all differences of race, color and denomination. Because love is the determining factor in life, it cannot be confined to the limitations of the human mind and experience. It must flow from the Christian in order to be seen, to inspire, to heal and to encourage. Our desire must be to know Christ better and to serve Him better in love.

Such a love cannot be created by human emotion and desire because God is its origin and source.

Lord, teach me to be strong and faithful in my love for You and also to love my neighbor as myself. Amen.

Bound to Christ

Who shall separate us from the love of Christ?

Romans 8:35

Paul asks a penetrating question here. He implies that nothing can separate us from the love of Christ. He even mentions things that could attempt to do so: trouble or hardship, persecution, famine or nakedness, danger or sword. He comes to the conclusion that nothing will be able to separate us "from the love of God that is in Christ Jesus our Lord" (Rom. 8:39).

God loves you. This truth should give you comfort, strength and encouragement. Although it is a fact that God's love surrounds you, many people do not experience it because they erect barriers against it. Break down those barriers so that you may experience God's love in your life daily.

Holy Spirit, make me aware of You residing in me, so that my life will reflect Your glory and love. Amen.

March 28

The Song of Love

If I speak in the tongues of men and of angels, but
have not love, I am only a resounding gong
or a clanging cymbal.

1 Corinthians 13:1

This chapter unlocks all the noble qualities of
love. Here, Paul speaks about the path of love.
He begins by saying that one can possess any
spiritual gift, but if it does not bear the stamp
of love, it is useless.

If love is not part of miracles, of sacrifice, or of
our spoken and intellectual gifts, then they are
fruitless. The gift of intellectual excellence without love leads to intellectual snobbery. Knowledge lit by the fire of love is the only kind of
knowledge that can save people. None of these
are worth anything if they do not go hand-in-
hand with true love.

*Lord, my God, I thank You that all the love in my life
is but a mere stepping stone towards You. Amen.*

March 29

Love Forgets about Self

Love does not boast.

1 Corinthians 13:4

Boasting is a negative form of love, called self-love. True love is selfless. It would rather confess unworthiness than boast of its own achievements. Some people give their love as though they were bestowing an honor on the receiver. That is not love; that is conceit.

The one that truly loves cannot stop marveling at the fact that there is someone who loves him. Love is kept humble in the knowledge that it could never make a sufficiently worthy sacrifice for the one it loves.

This also applies to our spiritual lives. We dare not accept God's love as a matter of course as if we deserved it. Such pride robs us of the blessing and spiritual growth that God has in mind for us.

Lord, keep me humble in my love, so that it does not become the cause of pride and arrogance. Amen.

March 30

Love Keeps No Record of Wrongs

Love keeps no record of wrongs.

1 Corinthians 13:4-5

Godly love does not hold on to every bad memory of people who have transgressed against it. Yet often, people do not want to forget their hatred and revengeful thoughts. They become collectors of grievances and this process poisons their souls and drives the love from their hearts.

Many people fuel their anger in order to keep it alive. They brood on the mistakes made against them until it becomes impossible for them to forget.

Christian love teaches the great lesson of forgiving and forgetting. If you keep a record of the wrongs committed against you, you are inclined to miss the noble, good and beautiful things in life.

Holy Spirit, grant me the heavenly gift of forgiving and forgetting. Amen.

April

Praying Power

The Holy Spirit and Prayer

Live by the Spirit, and you will not gratify the
desires of the sinful nature.

Galatians 5:16

Many of us desire to have a meaningful prayer
life; to set aside more time for God and grow in
our relationship with Him, but time and again
we fail.

To triumph over Satan's attempts to distract
us in our prayer time is not easy. Yet Jesus promised the help of the Holy Spirit to those who
embrace Him as their Lord and Savior. "The
Spirit helps us in our weakness" (Rom. 8:26).

Open yourself up to the influence of the
Holy Spirit, be obedient to His guidance, and
you will find that your prayer life will change
dramatically – for the better.

*Lord Jesus, let me always pray, give testimony, and
serve with love. Teach me to act in response to
the guidance of Your Spirit. Amen.*

April 1

Prayer: The Challenge

Being in anguish, He prayed more earnestly.

Luke 22:44

There are enriching moments in prayer when you experience glorious intimacy with God and are filled with inexpressible joy. But true prayer often has a seriousness that touches on the deeper issues of life.

When you pray that God will help you grow spiritually, or show you the right way to live, or use you in His service, you will experience the full impact of the challenge of prayer.

Such prayers are essentially between you and God, but you will soon discover that they touch other people as well. As God lays people on your heart, you begin to understand the responsibility of prayer. Sharing in this privilege strengthens you to live in love towards God and your fellow man.

Lord, I pray that my heart would be overwhelmed by the love of God so that I can truly love and pray for those around me. Amen.

Pray for Discernment

Your righteousness is everlasting and Your law is true.
Trouble and distress have come upon me,
but Your commands are my delight.

Psalm 119:142-143

The trials and tribulations of life often force us to turn to someone or something for help. The psalmist, however, knew it was best to turn to God for wisdom and discernment.

He asked of God, "Give me understanding that I may live." He knew that God's plan for his life would preserve him from wrongful actions and would destroy the path of the foolish. Therefore he chose to delight himself in God and to uphold His statutes.

God promises to grant us wisdom if we ask Him for it (James 1:5).

Pray to God for discernment and wisdom in your struggle and ask Him to teach you what you need to know so you can apply His wisdom to your situation.

Heavenly Father, I am Your redeemed servant and I ask for wisdom and discernment. Amen.

An Effective Prayer Life

Do not be anxious about anything, but in everything, by
prayer and petition, with thanksgiving,
present your requests to God.

Philippians 4:6

Of all the Christian disciplines, prayer is the most commonly practiced and the least understood. Prayer should not be regarded as a life jacket in desperate times or as a wish list.

We begin by establishing a relationship of prayer with God. Develop an understanding of the living Christ, study His Word and meditate on His presence.

Thank and praise God for the privilege of prayer, and then cast all your cares, fears, problems and requests on Him and ask Him to grant you what He knows you need, as well as the grace to handle any situation that might arise. If you do this, God's plan will soon begin to unfold in your life.

You grant us more than we could ever ask for. We
always have the blessed assurance of Your love
and know that Your promises hold good. Amen.

Prayer Is the Key

That they may have the full riches of complete understanding, in order that they may know the mystery of
God, namely, Christ, in whom are hidden all the
treasures of wisdom and knowledge.

Colossians 2:2-3

Many Christians are ignorant of God's boundless grace. Their need blinds them to the One
who could supply their needs if they would
only trust Him.

Time and again Scripture reiterates that God
is more willing to give than we are to receive.
We are constantly reminded that if we pray
and believe, we will receive that which we pray
for. Prayer is the key that unlocks the treasure
chambers of God.

How God is going to answer your prayers is
neither your responsibility nor your concern. A
simple childlike faith that looks to God and believes unconditionally that He answers prayer is
the kind of prayer that God answers with joy.

*Lord, thank You for the key of prayer with which
we can unlock Your precious blessings. Amen.*

What Is the Focus of Your Prayers?

"Since you have asked for this and not for long life or wealth for yourself, but for discernment in administering justice, I will do what you have asked."

1 Kings 3:11-12

There is a strong temptation to focus on "self" in prayer. Many people only come before God with lists of requests. The danger is that your prayers become self-centered and your gratitude to God and to others take a back seat.

Every prayer that you pray must echo the immortal words of Christ, "Not as I will, but as You will" (Matt. 26:39). This is the highest practice in faith – complete surrender to God's will and committing yourself to Him. In this way you acknowledge His sovereignty over your life and your circumstances.

Christ has His hand on you, and the Holy Spirit will guide you onto the perfect path.

*Lord, You guide me when words fail me in prayer.
Your mercy intervenes and gives me peace. Amen.*

April 6

Surrender Your Life to God

"Lord, teach us to pray."

Luke 11:1

Most Christians are very aware of their inability to pray according to the will of God. Christ sacrificed Himself for us. He gave Himself freely, but He will enrich your life only as far as you allow Him to.

The depth and quality of your devotion to Him will be reflected in the strength of your prayer life. It does not mean a thing to ask God for a meaningful and positive prayer life unless you do your share to develop it.

If you surrender yourself more completely to Christ, you will become increasingly aware of His living presence in your prayer life.

Lord, teach me not to fret about what tomorrow may bring. Teach me to quietly trust in You, because You are good and all-wise. Amen.

April 7

Be Fervent and Persevere in Prayer

So He left them and went away once more and prayed
the third time, saying the same thing.

Matthew 26:44

Some Christians wonder why, if God is all-seeing and omniscient, they still need to persevere
in the discipline of prayer. They feel guilty
about troubling God over and over with issues
that He is already aware of.

Remember, you often know about problems
in people's lives but you do not usually inter-
vene unless asked to do so. If you feel that a
particular matter in your life needs God's inter-
vention, do not hesitate to bring it before Him.
Remind Him of His promises and ask Him to
take care of the situation.

God will never tire of listening to you if you
come to Him in the name of Christ.

*In distress I call to You, O Lord, because only You can
grant me peace. Thank You for hearing my prayers
and for always answering my cry for help. Amen.*

Take Time to Pray

None of us lives to himself alone.

Romans 14:7

People always find the time to do the things they want to do, but are quick to find excuses for not doing the things they don't want to do. This happens in our spiritual lives too.

If you are making excuses as to why you can't pray or spend time with God, ask yourself why you are making these excuses. Why is your prayer life without power? Why has your faith become a burden instead of an inspiration of hope and faith?

This happens when you no longer reach out to God in prayer, or if you only ever express your personal desires. True prayer broadens your spiritual and intellectual horizons, and makes your relationship with the Savior more profound.

O Lord, please help me to develop a meaningful and powerful prayer life under the guidance of the Holy Spirit. Amen.

April 9

The Discipline of Prayer

Be anxious for nothing, but in everything by prayer
and supplication, with thanksgiving, let your
requests be made known to God.

Philippians 4:6 (NKJV)

A relationship of prayer is a process that is established and strengthened over many years. You have to develop an affinity for the living Christ by constantly acknowledging His holy presence in your everyday life. It is a process of growing closer to Christ. Only then will your prayer life become meaningful and fulfilling.

Prayer is not only talking to God, but also listening to Him. If we listen with our souls and our minds, God will talk to us through the Holy Spirit and reveal His plans for our lives. Prayer that results in obedience to His will transforms the act of praying into a pulsating and dynamic force in our spiritual lives.

Lord, I wish to glorify You forever, through Christ.
Through the guidance of the Holy Spirit, help
me to obey You in prayer. Amen.

Pray – Regardless …

When my life was ebbing away, I remembered You,
LORD, and my prayer rose to You, to Your holy temple.

Jonah 2:7

Many people deny themselves the privilege of
the peace of God, simply because they feel too
undeserving to talk to God.

Yet Jesus promised that He will not cast out
anybody who comes to Him. He also emphasized that He did not come to call the righteous,
but sinners, to salvation. Throughout the Scriptures you can read of His unfathomable mercy
and endless love that reach out to all people:
the good and the bad, the worthy and the unworthy.

However unworthy you may feel at this moment, reach out to Him in prayer and He will
take you by the hand – and nobody will snatch
you from Him.

*Father, I want to live my life glorifying You. Help me
not to lose sight of You when times are difficult. Guide
me towards obedience through Your Spirit. Amen.*

Pray without Pause

Pray continually.

1 Thessalonians 5:17

It is difficult to create a pattern of prayer in your life. It is even more difficult to cultivate a sustained prayer life.

The motive behind sustained prayer is to listen to God and to be sensitive to His guidance through the Holy Spirit. In the quiet of your deepest being you will feel His presence and experience His omnipotence. Regardless of where you may find yourself, or what you may busy yourself with, you can lift your heart to God, even for a single moment and in a fleeting thought, and in doing so, experience the reality of His presence.

Thank You, Lord, for hearing my prayers of supplication and thanksgiving, and that You bless those who wait on You in prayer. Help me to maintain a childlike trust in You – now and forever. Amen.

Prayer Is a Spiritual Discipline

After He had dismissed them, He went up on a mountainside by Himself to pray. When evening came, He was there alone.

Matthew 14:23

Everyone who yearns to develop a meaningful spiritual life must be willing to be disciplined. Without discipline faith has emotion, but lacks the quality for spiritual growth.

The most important component in the development of a stable and positive faith is the nurturing of a living and powerful prayer life. The Master, our Example in prayer, kept a conscientious watch over His times of personal prayer, even dismissing His most intimate friends to be alone with God. This means that your devotional appointments with your heavenly Father should be kept faithfully and conscientiously.

I call out to You, O Lord, and cast my sorrows, my doubts and my needs on You, because I know that You will hear my prayer. Amen.

April 13

Prayer Is Essential

Very early in the morning, while it was still dark,
Jesus got up, left the house and went off to a
solitary place, where He prayed.

Mark 1:35

Some of God's children are just too busy. Even if you are extremely busy in the service of the Lord but are not supported by the power of faithful prayer while you work, you run the risk of a complete breakdown and burnout of your spiritual life. You cannot fulfill your spiritual duty without prayer.

Prayer is the encouragement and inspiration for Christian service. It gives sincerity to everything that you embark on in the Master's name and gives you a deep satisfaction that you cannot get from any other source.

Father, through Your favor, may I experience more comfort in times of adversity, more sorrow over sin, more joy in my labors. May I be inspired by prayer and pursue Your example diligently. Amen.

Make Prayer Your Motivational Power

"When you pray, do not keep on babbling like pagans, for they think they will be heard because of their many words."

Matthew 6:7

There are many people who do not give serious thought to their prayers to God. They have a fixed pattern that used to be meaningful but through repetition has lost its meaning.

When you spend time in the presence of the living God, and you are sharing your wishes with Him, you must be seriously mindful of the guidance of the Holy Spirit. Ask Him while you pray if there is anything that you can do to make your prayer life more fertile. Believe in your prayers and then leave everything in God's hands and see how He works in your life.

Father, through Christ I wish to glorify You as my Father. Grant that I, through the guidance of Your Holy Spirit, may be obedient in my quiet times with You. Amen.

April 15

A Devotional Exercise

Be joyful in hope, patient in affliction, faithful in prayer.

Romans 12:12

Do you get the maximum spiritual satisfaction from your devotional time? How you answer this question reveals the difference between an ineffective prayer life, and one filled with an awareness of the presence of God.

In your everyday life, the opportunities for prayer become incalculable. Send up brief prayers for those who seem to be tired or disillusioned or pray thoughts of joy with those who are joyful. You need never be at a loss for things to pray for, provided you practice prayer in every situation of life.

By broadening your devotional base, your devotional times with God become more profound. While practicing praying for others, you are strengthening your ties with Jesus Christ.

Lord God, thank You that I may come to You in prayer
for advice and guidance. Thank You for Your Spirit
that teaches us to pray. Amen.

Be Patient in Prayer

I will stand at my watch and station myself on the ramparts; I will look to see what He will say to me, and what answer I am to give to this complaint.

Habakkuk 2:1

So often people complain that their prayers remain unheard. They become impatient with God and their faith weakens.

Yet it is an established and irrefutable fact that God hears and answers our prayers. However, we need to know His Word to understand that His answer comes in His perfect time, and in His perfect way, according to His perfect will. This is also done according to our needs – not our wishes and will, unless they are in accordance with God.

Truly effective prayer often requires us to watch and wait. He will reveal Himself to us and show us His way in His good time.

Father, grant that in times of doubt I will turn to You, that I will hold on to Your constancy and on to the assurance that I have in Jesus Christ. Amen.

April 17

Peace in Prayer

Devote yourselves to prayer, being
watchful and thankful.

Colossians 4:2

There are many people whose lives are ruined by anxiety, worry and fear. Paul says, "Do not be anxious about anything, but in everything, by prayer and petition, with thanksgiving, present your requests to God. And the peace of God, which transcends all understanding, will guard your hearts and your minds in Christ Jesus" (Phil. 4:6-7).

Especially in times of adversity, there is absolutely nothing that you can do in your own strength to solve your problem. Jesus said that without Him we can do nothing, but take heart because He also said that in God, all thing are possible.

How wonderful, Lord, that I may come to You when I am sad and when I repent of my sins. Thank You for hearing my prayers. Amen.

Wisdom Comes
through Prayer

*If any of you lacks wisdom, he should ask God,
who gives generously to all without finding fault;
and it will be given to him.*

James 1:5

Prayer holds many advantages for those who make it part of their daily routine. To wait patiently in the presence of God creates an opportunity to experience the Holy Spirit. It can transform a time of senseless words into a source of strength and wisdom that restores balance to your life.

God talks to you through prayer. Whether you are plagued by doubt or confusion, or whether you are finding it difficult to make a decision, the person who prays will be enlightened and guided. Prayer confirms the existence of God in your heart and brings with it a new experience of life and wisdom.

*Jesus, Savior, Your burden is light and Your yoke is
easy. Help me to take up my cross daily
and follow You. Amen.*

April 19

Miracles through Prayer

Praise be to the LORD, for He has heard my cry for mercy. The LORD is my strength and my shield; my heart trusts in Him, and I am helped.

Psalm 28:6-7

Despite the cynicism of our age, God can still perform miracles. Every time someone is healed in answer to prayer, God has performed a miracle. Every time we experience peace in our hearts after a time of tension and suffering, or when our grief finally becomes bearable – then a miracle has occurred.

Hand your problems over to God in prayer today and wait on Him in faith. If there is something you need to do, do it without delay. Do not let despair overwhelm you. In the right time and in the right way, God will answer your prayers and you will be astounded by the results.

My God and Father, I know that You are powerful and that You can do far more than I can pray for or think of because You are the Almighty. Amen.

Have Faith in Prayer

You do not have, because you do not ask God.
When you ask, you do not receive, because
you ask with wrong motives.

James 4:2-3

One of the most common complaints is, "God doesn't answer my prayers." Some people think it is because God is punishing them or because prayer is futile. To these people prayer has become a mere formality.

True prayer is to personally experience the presence of the living Christ in your quiet times and throughout the day. It is the joyous assurance that the Lord keeps His promises and that He lives in you and you in Him.

Such prayer becomes a faith exercise that teaches you that, as you lay your requests before Him, He will give you what you need according to His wisdom, and you will recognize and accept His answers.

Lord my God, it is with gratitude and humility
that I accept Your will for my life, for in You
is perfect wisdom. Amen.

April 21

The Prayer of Jesus

After Jesus said this, He looked toward heaven and prayed: "Father, the time has come. Glorify Your Son, that Your Son may glorify You."

John 17:1

In preparation for the suffering that Jesus knew He would have to endure in the days ahead, He prayed for God to be glorified in His body at the Last Supper.

How could a terrible death on the cross bring glory to God? Jesus explains in His prayer that God is glorified through the obedience of the Son. We seldom feel that our suffering and defeat could be to God's glory, yet we seldom look at things from a godly perspective.

God's glory is reflected in our deeds of love, obedience and loyalty. Follow Jesus' example today by praying that God will be glorified in your life and by your obedience.

Loving Father, help me to contribute to the glory of Your name by doing everything in obedience to Your will. Amen.

April 22

May You Be Equipped

May the God of peace, that great Shepherd of the sheep, equip you with everything good for doing His will, and may He work in us what is pleasing to Him.

Hebrews 13:20-21

The Bible often refers to the children of God as sheep that are totally dependent on the Shepherd for food and protection. Although we live in a society where individual performance is highly regarded, we should never think that we can be everything that Christ expects from us in our own strength.

We have been brought into a covenant with our Lord and with one another through the sacrificial blood of Christ. Pray that God will equip you, as well as the believers in your community and local congregation, to join forces in doing God's work.

Lord Jesus, our Good Shepherd, equip Your children so that they will want to do Your work together. Amen.

Prayer for Discernment

Trouble and distress have come upon me, but Your commands are my delight. Your statutes are forever right;
give me understanding that I may live.

Psalm 119:143-144

The trials and tribulations of life often force us
to seek help. We tend to look for a sympathetic
ear first but it is always best to turn to God for
wisdom.

The psalmist knew that God's plan for him
would preserve him from wrongful actions and
would destroy the way of the foolish. Therefore,
he delighted in God and committed himself to
upholding His statutes.

Perhaps you are also struggling with a difficult problem. God promises to grant us wisdom if we ask Him for it. Pray for discernment
in your struggles and ask Him to teach you so
that you may apply His wisdom to your situation.

*Heavenly Father, I am Your redeemed servant
and I plead for wisdom and discernment
in everything I do. Amen.*

April 24

Prayer for an
Important Decision

So they proposed two men. Then they prayed, "Lord,
You know everyone's heart. Show us which of these two
You have chosen to take over this apostolic ministry."

Acts 1:23-25

Important decisions cause most of us concern.
We spend hours brooding over the advantages
and disadvantages, when we should actually
just ask God.

The disciples faced an important decision.
As a group they nominated two people who
were sincere followers of Jesus, but they real-
ized that they did not know the hearts of the
two candidates – only God did. Therefore they
entrusted the final choice to God in prayer.

Whenever you need to make a decision, dis-
cuss it with God in prayer. Ask for His wisdom
and guidance; ask Him to reveal His will to you.

*Omniscient God, Help me to make decisions in
accordance with Your will. Amen.*

April 25

Come, Let Us Pray

There on the beach we knelt to pray.

Acts 21:5

There are people who believe that prayer should be limited to the church or to the privacy of an inner room. They regard any form of public prayer with uneasiness and even disapproval.

Yet prayer is as much a form of communication as a conversation is. Except prayer is a conversation between our heavenly Father and us. There is nothing more natural than this.

While you should never be too shy to pray, it is also necessary to be discreet in terms of the time and place you choose to pray.

Trust in the guidance of the Holy Spirit and your prayers will always be a blessing to you as well as to others.

O Hearer of prayers, thank You that I can draw near to Your sacred throne at all times and under all circumstances, and I know that You will always listen. Amen.

April 26

The Path of Prayer

"When you pray, do not keep on babbling like pagans,
for they think they will be heard because of their many
words. Do not be like them, for your Father knows what
you need before you ask Him."

Matthew 6:7-8

Repetitive prayers may be a good way to develop the spirit of prayer, but the Lord makes it abundantly clear that prayer becomes ineffective when it deteriorates into the mere recital of pretty phrases.

True prayer is more than words. It is an attitude of the spirit and mind that reaches out to God. Prayer is a two-way process. You tell God what you want from Him and He reveals to you what He expects from you. Prayer is not a series of empty words, but rather an increasingly intimate relationship with the heavenly Father and a sincere desire to do His will.

God and Father, grant me the true spirit of prayer so that my communion with You will become more and more profound and meaningful. Amen.

The Gracious Gift of Prayer

Devote yourselves to prayer, being
watchful and thankful.

Colossians 4:2

What value do you place on prayer? Do you regard it as a wonderful gift of grace from God, or as an unbearable burden?

The privilege of prayer is a special gift from God to us. It is God's personal invitation to you to enter into His sanctuary, to talk to Him and listen when He has something to say to you.

Prayer is a discipline that requires preparation and practice. Make time to come quietly into the presence of God. Focus your attention on Jesus. Listen and speak to God and thank Him for the gracious gift of His love for you. That will enable you to live in an atmosphere of peace and trust.

Lord, thank You for the privilege of being able to bring every aspect of my life to You in prayer. Amen.

April 28

Prayer Is Boundless

At Gibeon the LORD appeared to Solomon during the night in a dream, and God said, "Ask for whatever you want Me to give you."

1 Kings 3:5

Many people get irritated with long-winded people who obscure the real issue behind a flood of words instead of asking something outright.

A similar situation can arise in your prayer life. The Old Testament prayer warriors were completely open and honest when they spoke with the Lord. They did not hide or hold anything back. Their confessions were complete and revealing, their requests were real and humble.

When presenting your requests to the Lord, be specific and honest. Ask for the gifts of wisdom and discernment so that you can recognize and accept His answers.

I want to be completely open when I speak
to You about the situations I am facing today.
I need Your wisdom and discernment.
Please help me to do what is right. Amen.

Prepare Yourself for Life through Prayer

Pray without ceasing.

1 Thessalonians 5:17

The future is unknown but you can prepare for it by developing a healthy prayer life. This will provide you with strength in moments of weakness, and comfort in times of sorrow.

Many people will tell you that praying is a natural instinct. This may be true, but an effective prayer life is the result of a disciplined and sensitive attitude before God.

Share your joy with God in prayer while the sun shines and there will be no anxiety when the storm comes. You will merely share in the quiet conviction that God is in full control and that you have prepared adequately for every situation in life through prayer. God will do the rest!

How wonderful, heavenly Father, to praise and glorify You. I want to sing the praises of Your great love and faithfulness for all nations to hear. Amen.

May

Growing in Christ

Only Jesus

When they looked up, they saw no one except Jesus.

Matthew 17:8

Perhaps it is time to pause for a while and examine your spiritual journey under the guidance and leadership of the Holy Spirit. Put all preconceived ideas aside and open up your spirit to His guidance.

It is the all-important sovereignty of Jesus Christ that generates a living faith in your heart. Faith is powerless and meaningless unless it is grounded in Christ and if He rules as King in your life.

If you allow the Holy Spirit to work freely in your life, He will lead you into a deeper and more intimate relationship with Christ. Jesus will begin to occupy the central position in your life.

Desire of my heart, I thank You that my heart thirsts for You all the time. Protect me from anyone or anything that could draw me away from experiencing Your presence in my life. Amen.

Grow in Christ

He is the image of the invisible God.

Colossians 1:15

Paul says that Jesus Christ and the eternal God are equal – that the One is like the Other.

This truth stirs one's soul, and you may feel that such spiritual heights are beyond your reach. Jesus lived on such a high moral level, setting examples of how to respond in certain situations, that you cannot live up to His example on your own. Yet this truth can also inspire and elevate us.

The living Christ does not condemn people for their sins, but inspires them to reach unprecedented heights. Depending on the strength and intensity of our devotion to Him, we can, in a small way, become like Jesus. And that is God's purpose for your life.

Stand by me, Lord Jesus, help me to grow into the likeness of Your image through the power and guidance of the Holy Spirit. Amen.

Together with God

I can do everything through Him who gives me strength.

Philippians 4:13

The Holy Spirit of God, who fills God's entire Creation, can also live in your heart. Accepting this truth releases the power of God in your life. When you think of yourself as a part of God's revelation of Himself, you enter into an intimacy with Him that will bring strength, balance, and vitality to your life.

When you realize that God created you, and that you are governed by His Spirit, you can also realize that your life should live up to His expectations. You no longer live to please yourself, but rather to do His will.

Through the grace of God and His Spirit, you can live a life pleasing to Him through the strength of the Lord Jesus Christ.

Merciful Lord Jesus, I accept the gift of the Holy Spirit
and therefore I can enjoy intimate fellowship
with You, my Lord and my God. Amen.

May 3

Cultivating
Spiritual Growth

Instead, speaking the truth in love, we will in all things
grow up into Him who is the Head, that is, Christ.

Ephesians 4:15

Christianity without spiritual growth cannot bring a deep, true joy and satisfaction. When you received Christ into your life, you did not only accept a system of doctrines; you promised eternal faithfulness to Him because you believe in Him. You can only understand Him better if you share your life with Him, and stop focusing on yourself.

Growing in Christ is not an exercise meant to create a comfortable religious feeling far removed from the hard realities of life – it should rather inspire the believer to positive action.

Renew your prayer life; rediscover the Spirit of Christ in the Scriptures and see how growth in Christ will lead you to new dimensions of life.

Lord Jesus, make my faith a dynamic power through the renewal of my prayer life and Bible study. Amen.

May 4

Live for Christ

His divine power has given us everything we need for
life and godliness through our knowledge of Him who
called us by His own glory and goodness.

2 Peter 1:3

The call to live a Christian life rings out once
again, but some of us are so overwhelmed by
the intensity of the task that our faith falters because of our human weakness.

Yet we do not have to rely on our own abilities to serve God at all. Remember that Christ
will not call you to any form of service without
equipping you for it. He has set the example and
all that He expects from you is to follow Him.

If you commit yourself to Him and place your
trust in Him completely, He will provide you
with everything that you need to truly live.

*Heavenly Father, I dedicate myself to Your service
anew, in the certain knowledge that You will provide
everything that I need to live an abundant life. Amen.*

Reach for
Spiritual Maturity

When I was a child, I talked like a child, I thought like a child, I reasoned like a child. When I became a man, I put childish ways behind me.

1 Corinthians 13:11

Some people's spiritual journey can be compared to a rocking horse: there is a lot of movement, but little progress. They never achieve spiritual maturity because they allow grudges to poison them with bitterness. Allowing a grudge to fester could harm your spirit and hinder your spiritual development.

Today you have an opportunity to grow by God's grace, to put the negative behind you, and to reach for a future of exuberant spiritual growth. If you open your heart to the Holy Spirit's influence, He will help you to forgive and forget – allowing you to concentrate on the things that will bring you spiritual maturity.

Lord, I cannot do anything without You. Fill me with Your Spirit so that I can grow and experience fulfillment in You. Amen.

Spiritual Growth
Is Essential

I gave you milk, not solid food, for you were not
yet ready for it. For since there is jealousy and
quarreling among you, are you not worldly?

1 Corinthians 3:2-3

Many people believe that God is great and awesome. In faith they accept that He is love, but
refuse to allow Him to fill their lives with that
same love. He promised His power to all who
serve Him, but they remain weak and powerless. They say they believe in Him, but they
don't experience His loving presence.

The Christian way of life is meant to enrich
the life of disciples. When you start becoming
spiritually mature, you develop a greater love
for others. When the love of Christ saturates
you, negative attitudes such as pettiness, jealousy and strife are dissolved. And then you
can rise above this immaturity and enjoy the
solid food that the Holy Spirit gives.

Lord, I want to know more of Your love daily
so that I can love others in turn. Amen.

To Live for Christ

For to me, to live is Christ.

Philippians 1:21

Too many people live purposeless lives, passing through life with superficial goals. But this type of life cannot bring real satisfaction. Real joy and fulfillment come from having a goal in life that pleases Christ.

Your goal should be to live your life in God's grace, for His glory. You will not be a spiritual person only when the mood strikes you; your faith will remain constant in spite of your fluctuating emotions. Living for Christ means committing your spirit, soul and body to Him.

If you live for Christ, He will be alive to you and you will know the ecstasy of a life poured out before God as a thank-offering. Accept the gift of Himself in your life and allow Him to live through you. Then for you, to live is Christ and to die is gain.

Holy Jesus, live in me so that I will do
all things for Your glory. Amen.

A Growing Spirit

Your faith is growing more and more, and the love every
one of you has for each other is increasing.

2 Thessalonians 1:3

If you are not enjoying your spiritual experience, you have probably allowed stagnation to
rob you of your spiritual zest.

A vibrant and powerful spiritual life requires constant attention. There will never be a
point when nothing more is required from you.
The longer you walk with the Lord, the greater
your enthusiasm should be, and any tendency
to grow slack should be resisted with all your
might.

Your quiet times sustain and nurture your
spiritual life. When you start fading spiritually,
ask God for the wisdom and courage to confess
your negligence and weakness and to help you
do something constructive about it.

*Lord, You who are the True Vine, let me grow in You
so that I can bear fruit that will please You. Amen.*

A Balanced Inner Life

If any of you lacks wisdom, he should ask God,
who gives generously to all without finding
fault, and it will be given to him.

James 1:5

Many people believe that to live a truly spiritual life, you need to live in seclusion; where the realities of life are either ignored or forgotten.

However, the lessons Jesus taught along the dusty roads of Palestine were very spiritual, yet essentially practical. For Him, everything – every thought and deed – was an expression of His relationship with His heavenly Father. Therefore, true Christians do not divide their lives into compartments, because all of their lives should be an expression of the spiritual.

Christianity touches the realities of every day and enables you to look, to a certain extent, at other people's problems as God does.

*O Spirit, take control of my life and let everything I do
and say be an expression of my love for You. Amen.*

Growth through Truth

Instead, speaking the truth in love, we will in all things grow up into Him who is the Head, that is, Christ.

Ephesians 4:15

If you ignore or undermine the necessity of growth in your spiritual life, it will not be long before you start to suffer on the stormy seas of disappointment and despair. There must be growth and development or your spiritual life will flounder on the rocks.

God makes resources available to us to assist us in our spiritual growth, such as fellowship with believers, Bible study and good deeds, but we should guard against these aids becoming goals in themselves. These are simply the result of our relationship with God and can never be a substitute for our faith in Him.

There can only be spiritual growth if your main objective is to reflect the image of Christ more and more. This should be the heart's desire of every believing Christian disciple.

My Lord, let Your Holy Spirit take possession of me so that I will live for Your glory alone. Amen.

Christlikeness

What will be has not yet been made known. But we know that when He appears, we shall be like Him.

1 John 3:2

The goal of every Christian should be to become like Jesus. Unconditionally accepting the lordship of Christ is the beginning of a new and satisfying way of life. Because you belong to Him, your love and mental and spiritual energy should be focused on becoming like Him.

Of course trying to do this in your own strength will only lead to frustration and disappointment. Pray that God will give you His Holy Spirit to help you with this process.

When you are united with Him, your faith becomes alive and your whole life is lived in total obedience to Him. Having a dynamic faith and obeying Christ will help you develop a Christlike character.

Master, I ask that You would fill me with Your life and goodness so that I can be completely obedient to You in all things. Amen.

Maturity

Until we all reach unity in the faith and in the knowledge of the Son of God, and become mature, attaining to the whole measure of the fullness of Christ.

Ephesians 4:13

It takes time for intellectual and spiritual maturity to reach its full potential.

In your efforts to reach maturity, you should have something against which to measure your progress. The apostle Paul teaches that we should measure our progress against nothing less than the character of Christ. Although this is an impossible goal, to aim any lower is to accept a secondhand life.

However, never forget Jesus' love for you and that He identifies with you in your human frailty. God will give you the strength to lead a godly life if you confess your dependence on Him every moment of the day. Draw daily from the strength that He makes available to you.

Through Your strength, Master and Savior,
I can aim to follow in Your steps. Amen.

Let Others See Christ in You

He said to them, "Go into all the world and
preach the good news to all creation."

Mark 16:15

Christians need to be witnesses for Christ.
We must not be ashamed of our faith in Jesus
Christ. It is, however, important to know when
to speak and when to be quiet.

There is one sure way to testify about your
faith without offending other people, and that is
to follow the example of Jesus Christ. His whole
life was a testimony of commitment to His duty,
sympathy, mercy, and love for all people – regardless of their rank or circumstances. This is
the very best way to be a witness for Jesus.

Ask the Holy Spirit to guide you so that others will see Christ in everything you do and
say. In this way you will fulfill the command
of the Lord.

*Help me, Lord Jesus, to let the Holy Spirit live
through me in such a way that others may
know of Your love for them. Amen.*

May 14

Spiritual Growth
through Prayer

After Job had prayed for his friends, the Lord
made him prosperous again and gave
him twice as much as he had before.

Job 42:10

It is not hard to make enemies. But remember, it is always possible to turn an enemy into a friend – although this isn't easy, as forgiveness requires true greatness.

Only those who have undergone meaningful spiritual growth can transform enmity into friendship. One sure and practical way to turn enemies into friends is to pray for them. This may sound absurd but it is a truly wise act if you desire a pleasant life. Prayer changes your attitude toward people and events, and when this happens, the battle is just about won. With God on your side you will have the ultimate victory.

Dear Lord, help me to grow in You so that I may develop a forgiving spirit. You have forgiven me through Your grace. Help me to follow Your example. Amen.

May 15

Stand by Your Convictions

Simon Peter answered, "You are the Christ, the Son of the living God."

Matthew 16:16

Many people long for a stronger faith. At one point or another we all need to answer the question that Jesus asked Simon Peter, "What about you? Who do you say I am?"

To benefit fully from the Christian experience, and to know the fullness and abundance of the true life that Jesus offers us, you must have a personal knowledge of the living Christ. This does not only mean learning everything about Him; it means acknowledging Him personally and surrendering your life to Him.

Acknowledge Christ's sovereignty over all creation and abundant life will be yours. That is why Jesus came to this world.

Make me a prisoner of Your love, O Lord,
because only then will I be truly free. Amen.

The Power of
Inspired Thoughts

Above all else, guard your heart,
for it is the wellspring of life.

Proverbs 4:23

Our thoughts control our lives. If your spirit harbors thoughts of bitterness, hate and envy, your mind will be drenched with negative and destructive thoughts, and you will never experience the dynamism of the Christian faith.

By living in harmony with the living Christ, and allowing His Spirit to become an inspiration to your spirit, you can achieve the impossible. Embrace God's ways with joy, build a healthy and profound prayer life and engage in faithful Bible study. This will give your mind the inspiration and strength that is only experienced by those who have put Jesus Christ first in their lives.

Through Your enabling grace, Lord Jesus, my mind is open to the inspiration of the Holy Spirit. Amen.

I Long for Your Commands

Your statutes are wonderful; therefore I obey them. The unfolding of Your words gives light. Direct my footsteps according to Your word; let no sin rule over me.

Psalm 119:129-130, 133

There are times in life when we long for guidance; long for someone who clearly knows the road ahead, who can help us avoid the potholes and dead-end streets.

This is the kind of desire that the psalmist had for the Word of God – that it would lead him every step of the way. He knew that the Word would lead him to true joy.

In today's world it often seems easier to desire God's freedom than His commandments. But the psalmist understood that God's commandments would bring true joy to his life.

Reaffirm your desire for God's Word to be your guide through life, today. Pray that God will help you resist the specific sins that cause you to stumble often.

Lord of the Word, let Your commandments guide me in the right paths. Amen.

May 18

Nourish Your Soul

"I am the bread of life. He who comes to Me
will never go hungry, and he who believes
in Me will never be thirsty."

John 6:35

In order to achieve a healthy existence and meet
the demands of everyday life, food is essential.

Just as your physical body needs nourish-
ment, so too does your spiritual life. It is an
important and integral part of your existence on
earth, as well as in eternity. Make sure that you
maintain a sustained conversation with Christ
so that you can constantly draw on the strength
flowing from His everlasting reserves.

In this way you will ensure that your life
will be powerfully enriched, because Jesus is
living inside you through His Holy Spirit.

Lord, You are my daily bread and Your truth sets
me free. Thank You for presenting us with the
Word so that we may get to know You better.
Help me to find You therein. Amen.

Reach for the Sky!

I want to know Christ and the power of His resurrection and the fellowship of sharing in His sufferings, becoming like Him in His death, and so, somehow, to attain to the resurrection from the dead.

Philippians 3:10-11

Ambition is a commendable characteristic but there is one ideal in life that must overshadow all others: to live in the image of Christ. This must be the greatest ambition of every follower of Jesus and demands complete surrender and commitment

The pure joy of a life in Jesus Christ cannot be measured. Such a life is priceless and precious. However, this demands a sacrifice. A sacrifice of your thoughts and ambitions must be laid on the altar of the living Christ so that His life can be reflected in you. The abundance of life in Him will be more than enough compensation for your complete surrender to your Savior and Redeemer.

Lord, I want to follow You and devote my entire life to Your service. Amen.

Stand by Your Convictions

Do not conform any longer to the pattern of the world,
but be transformed by the renewing of your mind.

Romans 12:2

There are a number of people who do not remain true to their principles and instead bow to societal pressure, suppressing their ideals.

If you do this, you violate your God-created character. What you believe is of crucial importance and becomes the only way for you to achieve true freedom in life.

If you are true to yourself, you may be scorned and rejected, but you will enjoy the satisfaction of knowing that you do not live a double life. It is only when you are at peace with yourself, and when you strive to please God rather than your fellow man, that you will be able to live a life of quality and contentment.

*Bless our labor in You, Lord. Help us to be steadfast
and strong, filled with fervor towards You. Amen.*

Grow in Wisdom
by Serving God

The fear of the LORD is the beginning of wisdom; all who follow His precepts have good understanding.

Psalm 111:10

To be educated is definitely an advantage in life. However, you can be highly educated and still suffer from spiritual want.

For the Christian, sanctification must always receive priority over education. A person who is in the process of developing spiritually is closer to the heart of God and, therefore, he is more skilled in understanding God's ways.

A spiritual person has discovered the true Source of wisdom in life. There is purpose in his service to God. He possesses peace and inner strength born from the fellowship of the Holy Spirit, and lives his life in such a way that he gains deep-rooted contentment and inspiration from it.

Lord, help me to spend every day in fellowship with you and to experience the fullness of life. Amen.

May 22

Spiritual Growth
Does Not Come Naturally

*The mind of sinful man is death, but the mind controlled
by the Spirit is life and peace.*

Romans 8:6

Physical growth is nature's way of allowing your body to develop. Your spiritual nature needs to grow too. Many people ignore this important aspect of their lives because it cannot be observed or measured like your body can. Yet, that does not make it any less important.

The greatest Guide and Advisor that you could ever find is Jesus Christ. He is the revelation of the living God and therefore has a perfect understanding of the problems that you wrestle with. Having a desire for oneness with Christ and yearning for a deeper relationship with Him will result in spiritual growth if you surrender to God completely.

*I can do nothing without You. In You I can grow and
gain fulfillment. I wish to remain in You always. Amen.*

Spiritual Renewal
Is Essential

Those who hope in the LORD will renew their strength.
They will soar on wings like eagles; they will run and
not grow weary, they will walk and not be faint.

Isaiah 40:31

From time to time it is necessary to take a break in order to refresh yourself and prevent burnout. Jesus often withdrew Himself from the masses and from society so that He could be alone with His Father.

It is even more necessary for us to spend time with our heavenly Father. It is in those precious moments when you spend quiet time with God, that you will discover the work of the Holy Spirit in your life. He will fill the empty reservoirs of your life and you will return to the world refreshed, bearing testimony of Him with the new strength and energy that you have drawn from the Source.

*Lord, fill me with Your Spirit. I ask for comfort,
strength and guidance – all to Your glory. Amen.*

May 24

Reflect God's Glory

Be imitators of God, therefore, as dearly loved children.

Ephesians 5:1

Most of us have a role model to which we aspire to be like, whether it is a teacher, a parent, an employer or even a friend, we want to be like them.

Yet, there is a much better role model for us, a perfect role model for you and me – Jesus Christ. Never forget that He lived and worked just like us and was subject to all the temptations, frustrations, joys and sorrows to which you and I are subject to.

Allow the Holy Spirit to take control of your life and manage it in a way that is acceptable to God. Then you will display a measure of likeness to Christ that will glorify God.

Lord, transform me into Your image more and more.
Transfigure me so that I may become more like You
in my behavior, thoughts and words. Amen.

The Most
Important Exercise

"The good man brings good things out of the good
stored up in his heart, and the evil man brings evil
things out of the evil stored up in his heart. For out of
the overflow of his heart his mouth speaks."

Luke 6:45

It is the quality of your inner life, not that which you pretend to be, that is significant. For a while you may be able to present a false front, but a time will come when storm clouds gather and you will be put to the test.

Cultivating a practical spiritual life is the most important exercise that one can undertake. It influences every aspect of your life and creates moral stamina, which enables you to rise victoriously above inner weaknesses.

When you live in harmony with God and allow the Holy Spirit to work in you, you will experience a motivating force in your life that will be reflected in your behavior.

Lord, teach me to fix my eyes on You more and more.
I want to devote my whole life to You. Amen.

Aspire to That Which Is Noble

Finally, brothers, whatever is true, whatever is noble, whatever is right, whatever is pure, whatever is lovely, whatever is admirable – if anything is excellent or praiseworthy – think about such things.

Philippians 4:8

Life can be an unpleasant or an exquisite experience, depending on your attitude towards it. When you are confronted with the cruelty of life, it is all too easy to allow it to affect your nature and character.

It requires spiritual sensitivity to consistently appreciate the beauty of life. To appreciate God as the Creator of all that is beautiful and noble, look around you. You will discover Him in unexpected places: in the smile of a friend, the innocence of a child, even a subtle act of love. In numerous ways, you will begin to see the wonder and beauty of life.

I bring You humble thanks, O Savior, that through the presence of Your Spirit I can appreciate the beauty and grandeur of life. Amen.

Share in the Life of Christ

God, who has called you into fellowship with His Son
Jesus Christ our Lord, is faithful.

1 Corinthians 1:9

God has called you to share in the life of His
Son, Jesus the living Christ – granting us a
privilege beyond words.

But with this privilege comes responsibilities. Intimacy with the Father demands that the
holy characteristics of God must be revealed
in your daily life by love, honesty, selflessness
and the integrity of your purpose. If you walk
in the truth of this amazing grace, your understanding of God deepens and your vision of
what your life could be broadens.

Once you have this you will never again be
limited by secret fears and doubts. Instead you
will face the future with confidence in the strength
of the living Christ.

You are the True Vine that gives lasting life.
Keep me safe, inspire me and bless me so that
I will forever remain fruitful. Amen.

May 28

The Person
You Can Become

However, as it is written: "No eye has seen, no ear has heard, no mind has conceived what God has prepared for those who love Him."

1 Corinthians 2:9

There are two sides to your personality: the person you are, and the person you would like to be. If these are in conflict with each other, you will experience bitter frustration and disappointment.

There is no harm in dreaming about the heights that you can achieve, provided that you take steps to make your dream a reality. You have the potential for spiritual growth that is beyond your wildest imaginings.

Spiritual greatness can be yours if you live in harmony with God. Your whole life should respond to His love with joy and gratitude.

I pray for inspiration and strength to become all that You created me to be. Help me to grow in You day by day and to fulfill Your vision for my life. Amen.

In the Service of God

Do your best to present yourself to God as one approved, a workman who does not need to be ashamed and who correctly handles the word of truth.

2 Timothy 2:15

Some people work tirelessly for God, seldom leaving any free time for themselves. Have you become so involved in God's work that you've lost sight of what God wants you to do?

If you don't get "topped up" by God regularly, one day something will just wither in your soul, all Christian activities will cease, and a life that may have been of great importance to God is lost.

The most important duty of any Christian worker is to strengthen your relationship with God every day. If you are too busy to spend time with Him in daily prayer then you are simply too busy to be an effective servant for Him.

Loving Master, help me not to lose sight of the service You want me to do. Amen.

Renew Your Character

Therefore, if anyone is in Christ, he is a new creation; the
old has gone, the new has come!

2 Corinthians 5:17

Most people observe our characters and form
an impression based on what they see. Yet,
only a few people take the time to develop an
agreeable character.

Many people believe that a person's character
cannot be changed. This is not true. If this were
so, the redeeming love of Christ would have
been in vain. Sinners can change into saints and
unpleasant people can become amiable when
the love of Christ enters their hearts.

When you open your life to Christ, His influence is reflected in your life and a transforma-
tion occurs. You surrender yourself to the Lord
and through that, your character changes.

*Your love is always with me, Lord. Father, draw
me closer into Your circle of love every day.
I want to remain in You. Amen.*

June

Peace in God

It Is Well with My Soul

Why have you rejected us forever, O God? Why does
Your anger smolder against the sheep of Your pasture?

Psalm 74:1

There are many people whose lives fall apart,
and they feel abandoned and forsaken. Yet it is
not true to believe that God will ever forsake
you. He has promised to be with you always
and to never leave you (Heb. 13:5). He even
proved His unfathomable love by sacrificing
His only Son on the cross for us.

God has a divine purpose for everything
that happens in your life. Even when you are
the victim of adversity, don't despair. He wants
to use these circumstances to bring about His
perfect will in your life.

Be still, my soul, the Lord is on your side. Patiently
bear all sorrow and grief and leave all decisions in
His loving hands. When everything else fails,
You, Lord, remain faithful. Amen.

Light in the Darkness

To those who have been called, who are loved by God
the Father and kept by Jesus Christ: Mercy, peace and
love be yours in abundance.

Jude 1-2

It seems as if the world is in a perpetual state of
chaos. Lawlessness and violence are increasing,
and people live in fear and insecurity. What is
the solution to such a sad state of affairs?

There can only be one answer and that is to
turn to Jesus Christ. He has already conquered
this dark and hostile world and replaced fear
with love so that You can confidently place your
faith and trust in Him.

Believe in Jesus and His promises and He
will give you the blessing of His peace that transcends all understanding. Trust in Him and He
will lead you from the darkness into the light
of His immeasurable love for humankind.

*Thank You, my Lord and God, that You grant perfect
peace to Your children in this dark world. Amen.*

God Is with You

"The LORD your God is with you, He is mighty to save.
He will take great delight in you."

Zephaniah 3:17

When things go wrong in life it is easy to despair and become overwhelmed by a sense of complete helplessness and hopelessness.

If ever anything seemed hopeless, it was on the day of Jesus' crucifixion. The hopes and dreams of those who thought that He was the promised Messiah were shattered when He died on the cross. But then God intervened and miraculously turned apparent defeat into victory. The sorrowful Good Friday was transformed into the triumphant resurrection of the Easter Sunday – when Christ rose victoriously from the grave.

Whatever circumstances you might find yourself in, however dismal, always remember that God is with you and that He is in control of your circumstances.

Redeemer and Friend, thank You that I can be sure that God loves me and is always with me. Amen.

Peace and Prosperity

You will keep in perfect peace him whose mind is steadfast, because he trusts in You.

Isaiah 26:3

When our minds are focused on the love of God, we experience indescribable tranquility and peace of mind. When you trust God during every day, and through every problem, you will be able to enjoy His peace.

By focusing on Jesus Christ and the peace and prosperity that He gives, you are set free from worry because you know that God is in control of your life – therefore no person or circumstance can disturb your tranquility.

His love enfolds you and covers your loved ones as well. This freedom cannot be taken away by anyone or anything – simply because you put your trust in the Lord.

*I want to trust You with every aspect of my life be-
cause of Your great love. Then my heart will be filled
with peace and I will fear no evil. Amen.*

June 4

Omnipotent Protector

The Lord is my rock, my fortress and my deliverer;
my God is my rock, in whom I take refuge, my shield
and the horn of my salvation. He is my stronghold, my
refuge and my Savior.

2 Samuel 22:2-3

When we are afflicted and needy, the love and omnipotence of God protects us. We can overcome any challenge, adversity, and problem if we only steadfastly trust in His loving care and grace.

He will command His angels to watch over us and protect us from any danger. He enables us to think quickly and act wisely and this is our protection against attacks and temptations from Satan. Our ability to adapt to our circumstances, to always have a song in our hearts, and to be joyful regardless of the situation, protects us against loneliness and depression, filling our hearts and minds with peace and joy.

Father, thank You for giving me Your light and Your wisdom so that I can always do what is right. Amen.

Your Will Be Done

"Yet not My will, but Yours be done."

Luke 22:42

Many things come our way in life – unexpected disappointments and trials – and often we cannot see any reason for them. But whether they are major or minor problems, we need to handle them all.

The Lord's love for us is endlessly tender and encouraging. He wants us to trust where we cannot see, and it will not be a reckless leap in the dark, as sincere trust and faith says, "I know for certain that God's will is best for me." This kind of faith leaves the choice up to God, with the words His Son taught us, "Your will be done!"

Eternal God and Father, thank You for sending Your Son to come and teach me what it means to let Your will be done in my life. Let Your Spirit assist me in this. Amen.

Through Him
Who Strengthens Me

Blessed is the man who trusts in the LORD, whose confidence is in Him.

Jeremiah 17:7

Everybody is searching for peace. No one can avoid the strain of life or the severe stress it brings with it. Jesus radiated love, serenity and peace; no matter how turbulent or chaotic the circumstances were around Him.

This was the result of His intimate relationship with His Father. Jesus regularly withdrew in solitude to pray and pour out His heart to His Father. Then He was able to return to a stormy life with the peace of heaven in His heart.

Whatever life may have in store for you, you will be victorious in His strength because, "I can do everything through Him who gives me strength" (Phil. 4:13).

You are my Keeper, O Lord. I place myself under Your control and in Your care. That is why I am assured of Your peace. Amen.

Believe without Seeing

Therefore we are always confident.
We live by faith, not by sight.

2 Corinthians 5:6-7

When you are faced with difficult situations and problems, do you trust God to make everything work together for good?

Jesus came to confirm that God loves you unconditionally. His care, help and compassion are unquestionable. If you are sure of this, then you will be assured that Christ will not allow anything to harm you. He wants what's best for you. With this assurance you can trust God unconditionally in everything you undertake.

Lord, take me to the place where Your perfect peace surrounds me, and I trust You in all things. Amen.

Peace Amidst Chaos

In keeping with His promise we are looking forward to a new heaven and a new earth, the home of righteousness.

2 Peter 3:13

In times of crises many people tend to collapse in defeat against what they perceive to be impossible problems. But to everyone who believes in Him, Jesus offers a life of abundance.

The Lord offers you His Holy Spirit if you surrender yourself to Him. It is His Spirit who gives you the ability to handle life's problems successfully. Whatever your circumstances may be, remember that Jesus is constantly at your side, guiding you and helping you. Place your trust in Him as He leads you, and remember that He is guiding you toward God's eternal kingdom where there is only harmony and peace.

Beloved Guide, I know that this life's struggles and problems will soon pass, and then I will enter into the eternal peace of Your kingdom. Amen.

Peace in the Storm

While they were still talking about this,
Jesus Himself stood among them
and said to them, "Peace be with you."

Luke 24:36

The stress, horror and inner conflict we may experience in life causes our peace to disappear, leaving us moody and discontent.

That is why we need to develop inner reserves from which to draw strength in difficult situations. When things go wrong and stress starts to overwhelm you, purposefully refuse to be swept into its current. Guard against bad temper and irritability.

Deliberately choose to remain tranquil by controlling your thoughts. Spend some time in God's presence, reaffirm your dependence on Him, and soon your spirit will become calm and His peace will refresh your life.

Eternal God who gives me peace in Jesus Christ,
lead me to quiet waters where there is peace in
the midst of the bustle of life. Amen.

I Know for Certain

He will never leave you nor forsake you.

Deuteronomy 31:6

It is important to have someone you can rely on and turn to in times of trouble. Yet sometimes even the closest friends can disappoint you.

Our Lord and Master will never let us down, however. If you need comfort, the Lord will comfort you. If you need guidance, the Lord will guide you. If you need inspiration for a difficult task, the Lord will inspire you.

If the road ahead of you seems to be strewn with problems, concerns and troubles, then ask the Lord to help you and you will discover that He is as faithful as His Word promises.

God my Father, thank You that I have the assurance
that You will never leave me nor forsake me.
Forgive me for the times when I've failed
and disappointed You. Amen.

Take Your Worries to God

"Therefore do not worry about tomorrow, for
tomorrow will worry about itself. Each day
has enough trouble of its own."

Matthew 6:34

Many people like to sit and brood over their
problems. If we do this, we allow worry to
flourish and then we lose hope.

Write down your worries clearly and simply.
Then calmly pray about each one and scale them
down to their real size. Prayerfully confirm that
God is in control of every situation and that
worry will no longer affect your tranquility and
peace of mind.

The secret is to take your burdens to God
in prayer. If you take this step today you will
discover that you are prohibiting worry and
anxiety from clouding your future because you
will discover that Christ is all-sufficient for your
needs, today and tomorrow.

*Savior, I praise and thank You that You protect me and
lead me into a pleasant future. Amen.*

June 12

Peace in the Storm

You will keep in perfect peace him whose mind is steadfast, because he trusts in You.

Isaiah 26:3

If you allow your thoughts to dwell on the things that are happening in the world today, you run the risk of being caught up in a whirlpool of hatred, bitterness and fear.

Yet, when your faith threatens to falter, God gives you the power to believe that all things will work out for the good of those who love Him. Peace is the direct result of trust. When your faith in God is sure, you receive an inner calm that brings balance to your life. Put God first in all things and you will know His peace and joy, even in the most trying circumstances.

Almighty God, thank You that with You at the center of my life I fear no storms, not even problems as threatening as hurricanes. Amen.

Heavenly Peace

"Peace I leave with you; My peace I give you."

John 14:27

The peace that Jesus offers His followers differs from human peace and allows us to look at life through God's eyes. When we do this, the worldly things suddenly do not seem to be that important. What God thinks of you, and how you relate to God, forms the foundation for your peace.

We need His peace in our everyday lives as well as in our inner beings. The Lord does not want us to stress about what is happening around us. So in all the confusion and chaos of daily life, look away from the world and look up to God. He is waiting to grant us His peace and love.

Prince of Peace, thank You that I know for certain that You have not only redeemed me, but that You also grant me Your heavenly peace. Amen.

God's Peace Is Unfailing

Who is God besides the Lord? And
who is the Rock except our God?

2 Samuel 22:32

Often when people are experiencing problems, or if they need advice, they turn to a friend for help. But human effort always falls short.

If you find yourself in a difficult situation, don't underestimate the power and love of God. Complete healing flows from an absolute and unconditional trust in, and surrender to, the living Christ. It doesn't matter what your problem is, the only lasting solution is to be found in the unfathomable love which God, through Jesus, bestowed on humanity.

Never be too proud or too afraid to turn to Jesus. Lay all your problems at His feet. He gave His life for you and will grant you the healing balm of His peace.

I want to hold on to You, Lord, when the storm winds blow and I feel insecure. Grant me Your peace. Amen.

Peace Be with You!

For the sake of my brothers and friends, I will say,
"Peace be within you."

Psalm 122:8

The world has enough problems without us adding to them by engaging in bitter quarrels and harboring hurts against others. To enjoy life fully, it is essential that you live in peace with your fellow man – but you can only do that if you have peace within yourself.

During His earthly ministry, Jesus had to handle a tremendous amount of adversity and enmity. He endured mockery, hatred, humiliation, unfair criticism and rejection. But, He never allowed circumstances to get the better of Him.

This was only possible because He was at peace with God, with Himself, and with all people. Accept it and express it through your life and you will experience a life of harmony and peace.

Savior, because I found You, my life is filled
with an indescribable peace. Amen.

The Center of Christ's Peace

"Peace I leave with you; My peace I give you. I do not give to you as the world gives. Do not let your hearts be troubled and do not be afraid."

John 14:27

Few people can honestly say that they do not long for peace of mind and inner tranquility. The troubles and pressures of life can drive many to seek comfort in different things; be it tranquilizers, drugs, professional help or even alcohol. Others simply give in to despair and just go through the motions of life.

The only proven way to handle the problems and tensions of life is by having a faith that is steadfastly grounded in the living Christ. Hold on to Him in all circumstances, talk to Him and, regardless of how desperate your situation might be, trust that He is always with you. His peace will then fill your heart, helping you overcome all your fears.

Prince of Peace, please help me to turn to You first in everything that happens to me today. Amen.

Your Search for Peace

To whom He said, "This is the resting place, let the
weary rest"; and, "This is the place of repose" –
but they would not listen.

Isaiah 28:12

People today struggle with tremendous pressure and in such stressful times tend to become very weary.

That is why Christ invites us by saying, "Come to Me, all you who are weary and burdened, and I will give you rest" (Matt. 11:28). Yet, instead of accepting this offer, many of us still try to find man-made solutions to our problems in our own strength.

Regardless of how busy you are, you must make time to withdraw from the demands of the day and spend time quietly at the feet of the Master. Focus on Him and His love. Regardless of how demanding and frantic your life may be, in the quietness you will be strengthened by God's peace.

*I have such a need for Your rest, Lord. Help me to be
strengthened in the peace of Your presence. Amen.*

Freedom and Peace in Christ

Jesus replied, "I tell you the truth, everyone who sins is a slave to sin."

John 8:34

Many people are slaves to destructive habits and lead sinful lives that are devoid of beauty and liberty.

Unfortunately many people have accepted this bondage as a way of life. They are content to live an inferior spiritual life because they are oblivious to the freedom and peace that Christ offers.

When you accept Christ as your Lord, you enjoy a new freedom, and a new pattern of life begins. All bitterness dissipates in His glorious love. The Holy Spirit sanctifies your thoughts, words and actions. The freedom that Christ gives spans your whole life and is the only way to find freedom and joy.

By doing Your will, Father, my life will be filled with a peace that lasts forever. Amen.

Christ's Peace –
My Inheritance

"Peace I leave with you; My peace I give to you. Not
as the world gives do I give to you. Let not your
hearts be troubled, neither let it be afraid."

John 14:27 (NKJV)

This world's peace is a poor reflection of the
peace that God gives to His children. The peace
of God is the most wonderful peace imaginable.
It affects every area of our lives. It is constant
and does not change according to our moods.

But this peace requires a steadfast faith in
Jesus Christ, who is the source of this peace.
Such peace banishes worry, because that is the
weapon the devil uses to undermine our peace.
Jesus prohibits fear, because fear is the enemy
of all peace.

*I praise and thank You for the peace that conquers
the fear and anxiety in my life. Amen.*

God's Perfect Timing

"I am the LORD; in its time I will do this swiftly."

Isaiah 60:22

Very often we find it difficult to accept God's timing, but we must never get impatient with the fact that He does not always react when we want Him too.

It is wrong to try to subject the omniscient God to your timetable. We only see the circumstances and problems that weigh us down now, while God sees the bigger picture from an eternal perspective. God's timing is always perfect, even though it may not seem that way to you now.

When His will becomes our primary concern, then we will start to understand God's perfect timing and will no longer be subject to fits of anxiety caused by circumstances.

Lord, You are omnipresent. When I lose all hope,
You are there. Thank You that I may know that
my life is safe in Your hands. Amen.

God Enables You To Control Your Thoughts

You will keep in perfect peace him whose mind is steadfast, because he trusts in You.

Isaiah 26:3

Your thoughts are your servant. Your thoughts influence your deeds because what you think and believe is the result of your circumstances. It is therefore imperative to discipline your thoughts in order to have a positive and constructive disposition towards life.

The greatest force in a healthy and emotional life is allowing the Holy Spirit to take control of your thoughts. You can, through the strength that Christ grants you, control your thoughts, and in doing so, experience the peace of God. There will be moments of disruption when evil thoughts will try to re-establish themselves, but if you focus on God and give Him control, nothing will destroy your peace.

You are my only Savior. Help me to trust in God
as my shield against the Evil One. Amen.

The Blessing
of a Peacemaker

"Blessed are the peacemakers, for
they will be called sons of God."

Matthew 5:9

Peacemakers create healthy relationships. They are people in whose presence bitterness, hatred and unforgiveness simply cannot survive. They are children of God and aim to be at peace with all people.

To live in peace with friends is easy, but what about your enemies? Therefore it is peace at a risk: it includes peace with your enemies and persecutors.

Peacemakers are willing to venture something so that they can perform a deed of peace for the sake of Christ. To be a peacemaker is not a pious ideal or an unreachable dream; in Christ, it is an achievable goal through the help of the Holy Spirit.

Holy Spirit of God, enable me, for the sake of Jesus, my Lord, to be a peacemaker in this world. Amen.

The Lord Is My Shepherd

The LORD is my shepherd, I shall not be in want.

Psalm 23:1

Those of us who belong to the Lord do not need to face the future with fear, because our Shepherd is already there and He will walk before us every day, leading us to our eternal destination.

Do you feel unsure about the path you have to take? The Shepherd will guide you. Do you feel that you need spiritual food and strength? The Lord will provide an abundant feast of good things.

The psalmist tells us, "I shall not be in want." So I shall not be in want of anything that I truly need. For every phase of life, every circumstance in which I may find myself, I truly do not need to fear. God will certainly be there to carry me through.

Lord God, it is a glorious reassurance to me that
You are my Shepherd and that in Your hands
I am safe and secure. Amen.

June 24

Green Pastures

> He makes me lie down in green pastures,
> He leads me beside quiet waters.
>
> Psalm 23:2

It is a blessed assurance to know that an omnipotent and loving God guides you from day to day. The Lord does not promise that all the pastures will always be green – sometimes they will be barren and desolate. He has also not promised that the waters will always be tranquil – sometimes the waves will break turbulently over us and the sky will be covered with ominous storm clouds. But the promise is that God, in His time, will bring us to green pastures and quiet waters.

If we put our childlike and unconditional trust in Him, we may rest assured in the knowledge that God will guide us in our everyday lives.

Lord Jesus, Shepherd of my life, thank You that I may
be safe and secure in Your care. Help me to accept
Your guidance at all times. Amen.

The Lord Guides Us

Then the disciple whom Jesus loved
said to Peter, "It is the Lord!"

John 21:7

When the disciples beached at dawn following a night of fishing, they recognized Jesus on the shore. He had prepared a meal for them. This tells us of the Lord's care – even after His resurrection He stayed close to His children.

We will get rid of a multitude of anxieties and confusions if we only recognize the Lord's hand in our lives and know for certain that He is by our side in every situation.

We know that He guides us on the path that is best for us. If we meet Jesus with unfailing certainty every day on our path through life, then we are amongst the most fortunate of all people on earth.

I praise and glorify You, Lord Jesus, because I see Your hand in every situation in my life and I know for certain that You will never forsake me. Amen.

The Gift of Peace

"Peace I leave with you; My peace I give to you."

John 14:27 (NKJV)

Jesus promises peace to His followers. Often God's blessings and peace are all that we desire here on earth to help us in our everyday lives.

The Lord does not want us to worry or lose hope because of things that are happening around us. That is why He promises to "bless His people with peace" (see Ps. 29:11).

The Lord does not force His gifts upon us, but He is always ready to grant them when we are ready to receive them. If we ask for peace in prayer, then the Lord will bless us with His peace in our innermost being so that we may experience His peace here on earth.

Savior and Prince of Peace, thank You that I know for certain that You have not only redeemed me, but that You have also granted me Your heavenly peace. Amen.

Shelter from the Storm

He who dwells in the shelter of the Most High
will rest in the shadow of the Almighty. I will
say of the Lord, "He is my refuge and my
fortress, my God, in whom I trust."

Psalm 91:1-2

Our lives can only be safe if we trust in the
Most High. His protection is not limited to certain times of the day; rather we are under God's
protection every moment of the night and day.

You need not fear anything – not the dangers of night or the attacks of day, not illness
and plague, nor war and fighting. God is with
us everywhere – at home, on the roads, even in
the workplace. With His protection and presence you will be able to conquer all dangers.

Take shelter under God's wings and be assured that you have a safe refuge where true
peace and safety can be found.

*God of Ages, Your children have always found shelter
and protection in You. Thank You that I know for certain that I will also find it when I come to You. Amen.*

Feast of Peace

"I am leaving you with a gift – peace of mind and heart.
And the peace I give is a gift the world cannot
give. So don't be troubled or afraid."

John 14:27 (NLT)

In a world that is so chaotic and conflicted, it seems naively idealistic to talk about peace. But peace is one of the gifts that God offers us through Jesus Christ. It is an eternal truth that all who love and serve God will experience His peace in their personal lives.

For those who have God's peace, it does not mean that they will escape the problems and sorrows of life, it means that they possess something more precious than the spirit of the times in which we live.

Christ's peace is not a passive quality that shuts our eyes to the harsh reality, but creates a positive approach to life, based on the belief in the trustworthiness of God.

Praise the Lord! Jesus, You came to bring peace.
Thank You for the peace of this glorious
truth ruling in my own heart. Amen.

Relieve Anxiety

"Do not worry about tomorrow, for
tomorrow will worry about its own things.
Sufficient for the day is its own trouble."

Matthew 6:34

In times of pressure and stress – when it feels as if hope is dying – anxiety takes root in your heart and mind and flourishes. Anxiety is the product of a confused mind and little faith.

One way of overcoming a feeling of anxiety is to determine its cause. For many people their anxiety is vague and indefinable, but it continues to erode their spirit and mind – with disastrous consequences. Take your anxieties to God and ask Him to be Master of the situation. If you do this, you are no longer allowing the Devil to attack your calm approach to life or allowing anxiety to spoil tomorrow.

Holy Spirit of God, help me not to be anxious about
tomorrow, because You have every day in Your eternal
and loving hand. Amen.

July

Hope and Trust

A New Hope

Trust in the L{\scriptsize ORD} with all your heart and lean not on your own understanding; in all your ways acknowledge Him, and He will make your paths straight.

Proverbs 3:5-6

The decisions you make on a daily basis could have far-reaching consequences for your life. Spend some time in God's presence today and seek His will. This will lay a solid foundation for a life built on trust in the living Christ.

God will never disappoint you. Through the Holy Spirit, He will open up new horizons of what life can offer. Your values will change as you start looking at life through His eyes.

The more closely you walk with Him, the more clearly you will understand all that He can do in and through your life. Resolve to strengthen and enrich your relationship with Christ so that you can blossom and be as fruitful as He desires you to be.

Loving Lord, I come before You in earnest prayer, asking that my imperfect life might reflect something of Your holiness. Amen.

Hope for the Future

Has He not made with me an everlasting covenant,
arranged and secured in every part?

2 Samuel 23:5

Many people look to the future with deep anxiety because they are carrying the heavy burden of their daily responsibilities alone. Unless you have a strong faith, this could have far-reaching effects on your physical, emotional and mental well-being.

The Son of the Most High God died and rose from the dead to set you free from this burden of worry. God loved you so much that Jesus Christ gave His life to redeem you from the terrible burden of anxious worries. Unlike those who have no hope, you are blessed with the assurance that the Savior died in order that you may live. Regardless of the circumstances you're in, this assurance should be a great comfort and encouragement.

*I thank You, Lord, that in spite of my
circumstances I can praise You, for You are
in control and You are ever-faithful. Amen.*

Living Hope

Praise be to the God and Father of our Lord
Jesus Christ! In His great mercy He has given
us new birth into a living hope through the
resurrection of Jesus Christ from the dead.

1 Peter 1:3

Let your anxious heart rejoice with the glorious expectations of all the riches and treasures that await you in heaven. Thank God for such a hope and turn your thoughts away from all the burdens and worries of the world. Renew your mind with thoughts of the pure untainted inheritance that is waiting for you – an inheritance that can never be destroyed.

Prayer focuses our hearts on heaven while our feet remain firmly planted on the earth. So even if you are involved in a bitter struggle here on earth, remember your inheritance in heaven and praise the Lord.

I thank and praise You, Holy God, for all the treasures that You have set aside for me in heaven. Amen.

Trust God

I heard, but I did not understand. So I asked, "My lord,
what will the outcome of all this be?"

Daniel 12:8

People often find it difficult to understand God's
purpose for their lives – especially when things
go wrong. Their vision of the future fades and
their faith wavers.

The core of a strong faith depends on your
ability to trust God completely, no matter what
happens. The true test of faith comes when
things turn against you; when you are tempted
to question God; when you are in total despair.

Jesus had an unconditional trust in God.
Even in His darkest moments, His faith was
strong enough to enable Him to fulfill the will
of the Father. Trust God in all circumstances and
the grace of God will help you deal with every
situation.

*Lamb of God, I look up to You to strengthen my faith
through the work of Your Holy Spirit in my life. Amen.*

Trust in God

Though an army besiege me, my heart
will not fear; though war break out
against me, even then will I be confident.

Psalm 27:3

Like never before, people are worried and anxious about what the future holds. It is essential for people to have a spiritual foundation upon which to base their hopes and expectations. Unless you have a positive trust in a power greater than yourself, the future will be filled with uncertainty for you.

Faith in God must be intimate and personal if it is to give you hope for the future. The omnipotent Creator God has not abandoned this world despite appearances to the contrary. His master plan will still be carried out, just place your trust in Him and meet the future with the serenity He will give you.

Savior and Lord, I live from day to day trusting Your very real presence and omnipotence in this world. I do not fear because You are my refuge. Amen.

On Eagles' Wings

Those who hope in the LORD will renew their strength.
They will soar on wings like eagles.

Isaiah 40:31

Too often we get hung up on things that don't really matter and we allow them to distort our view of life.

A positive Christian, however, has the ability to rise above small irritations by trusting in the Lord in all circumstances and by always remaining conscious of His presence. It is impossible to be trivial and small-minded when the love of Christ fills your heart and mind.

Spreading God's love by the power of the Holy Spirit means being able to rise above trivialities and reach the heights that the God of love desires from all His children. Then we can rise up on the wings of eagles and see things from their true perspective.

Holy Spirit, fill me with Your presence and help me to trust in God so I can rise above my problems. Amen.

July 6

Unshakable Trust

Be joyful in hope, patient in affliction.

Romans 12:12

When everything seems to be going wrong you may feel overwhelmed by your problems and want to give up or try to solve them in your own strength. But remember, the Lord has promised to never leave nor forsake you.

However, you must have patience because you cannot hurry or prescribe to God. He does everything in His own perfect time and way. God sees the big picture of your life – He is all-knowing and all-seeing.

Ask the Holy Spirit to teach you to wait patiently on the Lord. Then, with childlike trust, you can leave everything in God's hands. Those who stand steadfast in affliction receive God's most precious gifts from His treasure house of mercy.

Lord and Father, I find peace of mind in trusting You completely. Amen.

Holy and Omniscient

The LORD has established His throne in heaven,
and His kingdom rules over all.

Psalm 103:19

In adverse circumstances, people often start to doubt God's power and majesty. Their faith often wanes and the obstacles of life cause them to stumble.

When you find yourself surrounded by difficulties, hold on to your faith and put all your trust in the victorious Christ. In all the centuries since Creation, there has not been one instance where the righteousness of God did not triumph over evil.

This same God wants to be your daily companion. He reigns supremely over everything and everyone. Let this be your source of strength and power in life, with all its problems and demands.

*Father, I find strength and inspiration in
knowing that You are with me, and that Your
righteousness prevails in every situation. Amen.*

July 8

Facing the Future

Surely God is my salvation; I will trust and not be afraid. The LORD, the LORD, is my strength and my song; He has become my salvation.

Isaiah 12:2

If you are fearful and worried about the future, you will project the very things that you fear and wish to avoid, into your future. Like Job you will then find yourself saying, "What I feared has come upon me" (Job 3:25).

A sure way of increasing your hope is to work hard at maintaining a positive faith in Jesus Christ. Strengthen the ties that you have with Him until He becomes a living, dynamic reality to you.

The more real He becomes to you, the more your fears, which have undermined your trust in Him, will be transformed into a steadfast, constant faith in the Lord. Then you will be able to venture fearlessly into the future.

Holy Master, give me hope and confidence in the future as I walk with You. Amen.

Trust God in the Darkness

Yea, though I walk through the valley of the shadow
of death, I will fear no evil; for You are with me;
Your rod and Your staff they comfort me.

Psalm 23:4 (NKJV)

Every follower of Jesus faces days where his or
her spiritual life seems mediocre and their enthusiasm is dampened by indifference.

If this is you, then you need a fresh experience with God to drive the darkness from your
life. No matter how your feelings and emotions
change, God's love for you remains steadfast,
strong and secure. He loves you with an everlasting, unceasing love, and, even though you
feel far from Him, He is always close to you.

One of the benefits of going through dark
times in life is to appreciate the light and sunshine of God's love when we experience it
once again. God is able to use even the darkest
experiences on your earthly pilgrimage to the
benefit and blessing of others.

*Please hold my hand, Lord. I know that You will lead
me into the future one step at a time. Amen.*

A Life Based on Trust

I have learnt to be content whatever the
circumstances. I know what it is to be in need,
and I know what it is to have plenty.

Philippians 4:11-12

As a follower of Christ you have powers at your disposal that enable you to tackle life positively and constructively. Remember that dynamic discipleship is based on faith that finds expression in deeds, not in feelings. Focus on the fact that God loves you, even though you might be experiencing the darkest time of your life.

Acknowledge the fact that He will never leave you, even though you may not be able to feel His presence right now. If your life is based on your faith in Christ, your confidence will increase and you will overcome every feeling of inferiority. There will be no situation that you will not be able to handle through Christ's wisdom and power.

I thank You, Lord Jesus, that I can start every day with confidence because I find my strength in You. Amen.

Faith Requires Trust

"Master, we've worked hard all night and haven't caught anything. But because you say so, I will let down the nets."

Luke 5:5

The disciples had labored hard throughout the night without catching any fish. They were experienced fishermen and knew there were no fish to catch. Yet, at Jesus' words, they let down the nets once more. According to the Scriptures they caught so many fish that the nets began to tear. And so their faith was rewarded.

When you lay a matter before God you should trust Him so much that you are willing to accept His will and be obedient to the prompting of His Spirit no matter what. Forget about what others think or say; trust God unconditionally and He will reward your faith.

I place my trust in You completely, Lord Jesus, in the knowledge that You will never disappoint me. Help me not to disappoint You through my unbelief. Amen.

Trust in God

Let us hold unswervingly to the hope we profess,
for He who promised is faithful.

Sometimes everything in your life looks hopeless and bleak. Your dreams have been destroyed, your hope has died, and nothing seems to be working out right. In such a depressed state we become easy prey to the Devil, whose main aim is to drive a wedge between our heavenly Father and us.

When you feel dejected, remember that Jesus has promised to be by your side throughout your life. He invites you to cast your problems on Him and to trust Him in times of distress. Study the Gospels, see how compassionate and loving Jesus was towards people, and draw hope and comfort from that.

Thank You, Lord Jesus, that even when I feel dejected, You are always by my side. Lift me from the well of misery and let me sing a song of praise once more. Amen.

The Richness of Life

Not that we are competent in ourselves to
claim anything for ourselves, but our
competence comes from God.

2 Corinthians 3:5

If you are searching for the deeper meaning of
life, you are on an exciting journey. Fix your eyes
beyond the temporal, and discover that you are
an eternal being created in God's image.

God gives purpose to your days and motivation to live life to the full. As you yield to
the control of the Holy Spirit, you will become
more and more aware of how magnificent life
truly is.

If we would only surrender to God without
restraint we would see His glory and omnipotence and we would experience the richness of
life in all its facets.

*Great and mighty God. I praise You for revealing Your
greatness to me and enriching my life through it. Amen.*

July 14

Grace and Peace in God

I lie down and sleep; I wake again,
because the LORD sustains me.

Psalm 3:5

How do you prepare yourself to handle any situation that might arise so that you can ensure a peaceful and safe life? History reveals that people who walked intimately with God found hidden resources of strength to overcome their adversities.

Those who have an unflinching faith in the living Christ and put their trust in Him will not waver or break under attacks, they will not give in to the icy touch of fear.

The same Christ who hushed the wind and stilled the storm at sea, is calling out to you today, "Be strong and courageous. Do not be afraid" (Deut. 31:6). Put your trust in God and see for yourself how His love and grace cause the storms in your life to subside.

O Lord, help me to trust You and have unflinching faith in the midst of the storms of life. Amen.

July 15

Light in Times of Darkness

Even in darkness light dawns for the upright, for the gracious and compassionate and righteous man.

Psalm 112:4

Every believer must accept that there will be times when dark clouds of affliction will cover your path. At first God is such a glorious reality to you and joy floods your life, but the clouds of despondency will soon appear.

When that happens, it is essential to re-establish the truth that God is unchanging; His love for you is exactly what it has always been. You may find the darkness hard to accept and God may seem far off, but hold on steadfastly to the assurance that God loves you and that He cares for you.

Fortunately the dark times do end and you will step out of the shadows with new strength and walk in God's sunshine again.

I will trust You in the darkness, because I know that You are good. Amen.

Plan with God

> So that your faith might not rest on
> men's wisdom, but on God's power.
>
> 1 Corinthians 2:5

Have you ever experienced the disappointment of seeing carefully planned dreams fall apart? Many people who experience such a setback are unwilling to take any other risks.

Don't let that happen to you – don't let your potential lie wasted and unused. When you trust God in everything you do and submit to His will and obey Him, you might feel that things move too slowly for you, but be patient. Steadfastly put your trust in God and you will find peace of mind knowing that God is in control and that the fulfillment of your plans will be to your lasting benefit.

Lord, I know that when I bring my plans for my life to You, You will show me what Your plans are, and You will help me to succeed in all things. Amen.

On the Wings of Eagles

Those who hope in the LORD will renew their strength.
They will soar on wings like eagles.

Isaiah 40:31

It is easy to get burdened by all the pettiness in life. Some issues are of little importance whilst others are mere molehills that we turn into big mountains.

Do not allow circumstances to claim so much of your attention that you lose sight of spiritual realities. These are the very things that add depth, purpose, meaning and direction to your existence.

By developing a consciousness of the presence of the living God, and by always trusting in Him, you will be able to see things from His perspective instead of from the world's.

Holy Spirit, fill me with the love of the Father and of the Son and of the Spirit so that I can love others with Your love and so demonstrate my faith in You. Amen.

July 18

Your Divine Companion

The righteous cry out, and the LORD hears them; He delivers them from all their troubles.

Psalm 34:17

Many people struggle with loneliness for a variety of reasons. When you find yourself feeling depressed and lonely, Satan will try to sow seeds of doubt, discouragement and despair in your heart, making you want to give up hope.

But don't give up! The hand of God rests on you always. Rather lay your fears and worries at the feet of the living Christ. Open up your heart and life to the Holy Spirit and He will fan the flame of hope once more, allowing it to burn brightly and light your path.

Powerful Redeemer, grant me the strength to keep my hand firmly in Yours even under the most difficult circumstances. Lead me from the darkness into Your wonderful light. Amen.

Light up Your Life

When Jesus spoke again to the people, He said, "I am the light of the world. Whoever follows Me will never walk in darkness, but will have the light of life."

John 8:12

Darkness can cause fear, depression, loneliness and sorrow. The darkness of the soul has a similar effect on people. When light comes, it brings relief and a feeling of safety.

The light of hope and peace flickers and dims when we face afflictions and trials. The only way to overcome the darkness is to turn to Christ. Instead of fearing the darkness, light a small candle of faith to brighten it.

Walk in His light and soon you will find that the darkness has passed. With His light in your heart, each day becomes radiant for you.

Loving Guide, while You hold my hand I am safe and secure. Strengthen my faith daily. Amen.

God Is with You

The LORD your God is with you, He is mighty to save.
He will take great delight in you, He will quiet you with
His love, He will rejoice over you with singing.

Zephaniah 3:17

When things go wrong in your life it is easy
to lose hope. Especially when the battle you
are fighting seems so unfair. Even people who
seem invincible in the beginning, might later
be overwhelmed by a spirit of helplessness and
hopelessness.

Whatever circumstances you find yourself
in; however dismal the future may seem; despite all the problems you are facing, remember that God is with you and He is in control of
your circumstances. Trust in Him and He will
grant you victory, even when everything seems
hopeless.

*Redeemer and Friend, thank You that I can be sure
that God loves me and is always with me. Amen.*

God's Sufficient Grace

"My grace is sufficient for you, for My power is made perfect in weakness."

2 Corinthians 12:9

All of us, at one point or another, when faced with a certain situation feel hopeless and defeated.

Yet whatever the predicament you are in, however dark the outlook, never underestimate the extent of God's love for you and the expanse of His grace. Look at examples in the Bible or in history when God transformed despair into hope and defeat into victory through His grace.

He is waiting for you to turn to Him and trust in Him. Your faith will be rewarded and, in His own wonderful way, He will deliver you.

God, through the years You have proved Yourself to be faithful. Therefore I will hold on to Your hand in the future because Your grace is sufficient for me at all times and under all circumstances. Amen.

Love Fills the Heart with Hope

Brothers, we do not want you to grieve like
the rest of men, who have no hope.

1 Thessalonians 4:13

Hope and despair are found in the hearts of people and not in circumstances. Love is so important because it causes hope to triumph. When things are at their darkest, hope rises through love to light the darkness of night. There is no room for despair; God has enough love to avert it. He has woven hope into the nature of man so that we can trust in the future.

When all is hopeless, it is hope that keeps us going. Hope strengthens the soul so that we can hold on to eternity and on to the love of God. His love is infinite; He gives us hope out of love.

Lord, may I never believe that anyone is hopelessly lost, because, in love, You sent Your Son to save the lost. Amen.

Walk in the Light

This is the message we have heard from Him
and declare to you: God is light; in Him
there is no darkness at all.

1 John 1:5

Many things that happen in the world today
are symptoms of a sick society. The average
person feels unable to confront the evil around
him or her, which can give rise to an attitude of
complete despair.

Nothing in our modern world can be as ap-
palling as the crucifixion on Golgotha. And yet
the Light broke through that darkest moment
in history, when Jesus overcame the forces of
evil and rose triumphantly from the dead.

Regardless of how dark your circumstances
may be, put your trust in Christ, follow Him
and you will see how His light expels the darkness from your life.

Lord Jesus, in Your light we can see light. Help us to
see Your light in this dark world so that the darkness
will be dispersed. Amen.

Living Hope and Faith

Praise be to the God and Father of our Lord
Jesus Christ! In His great mercy He has
given us new birth into a living hope through
the resurrection of Jesus Christ from the dead.

1 Peter 1:3

Let your anxious heart rejoice with the glorious
expectation of all the riches and treasures that
await you in heaven. Thank God for that and
let this prayer help you to turn your thoughts
away from all the burdens and worries of this
world.

Renew your mind with thoughts of the pure
unblemished inheritance that is waiting for you –
an inheritance that cannot be destroyed. Though
we may face bitter struggles here on earth, we
have an inheritance waiting for us in heaven.
That's worth feeling hopeful and praising God
about!

*I thank and praise You, holy God, for all the treasures
that You have set aside for me in heaven. Amen.*

I Will Always Have Hope

As for me, I will always have hope; I will praise You more and more. My mouth will tell of Your righteousness, of Your salvation all day long.

Psalm 71:14-15

What an incredible privilege it is to tell others of the wonderful things that God has done for you. Recall God's protection and guidance in your life and tell someone about how He has helped you in the past.

Place your trust and hope in God. Believe that He will never leave you but will strengthen you and be with you in every time of trial and affliction. Let the psalmist's praises be your example and may you also have such a passion to declare the praise of God as long as you live.

Loving Master, I am overwhelmed at all that You have done and I want to be a witness to Your goodness to everyone I meet. Amen.

Open the Eyes of My Heart

I pray also that the eyes of your heart may be
enlightened in order that you may know the
hope to which He has called you, the riches of His
glorious inheritance in the saints.

Ephesians 1:18-19

At the time of writing this, Paul was confined to
a prison cell in Rome, under the constant watch
of the Roman guard. But who could possibly
tell from his prayer that anything was wrong!
Paul's faithful description of God's power does
not allow even a hint of hopelessness or despair
to filter through. Instead he talks of the "glorious inheritance" of a future in heaven.

Paul's eventual hope was not in earthly
people, but in heaven, eternity and God. The eyes
of his heart could see clearly. Are the eyes of
your heart open?

*Wonderful Redeemer, help me, through Your Holy
Spirit, to grasp the wonderful future that You have
made possible for me. Amen.*

Praise the Lord,
All You Nations

"Praise the Lord and sing praises to Him, all you peoples." May the God of hope fill you with all joy and peace as you trust in Him, so that you may overflow with hope by the power of the Holy Spirit.

Romans 15:11, 13

We praise and honor the birth of David's descendant, our Lord and Savior, Jesus Christ. We place all our hope in Him for our salvation. Pray daily that you will find hope and peace in Him.

"May the God of hope fill you with all joy and peace as you trust in Him, so that you may overflow with hope by the power of the Holy Spirit." What a blessed way for one person to greet another!

Take time out today and thank God for His hope and allow it to spill over into every aspect of your life.

Lord Jesus, may all people on earth experience Your hope, peace and joy today. Amen.

July 28

Trust in God Alone

In Him our hearts rejoice, for we trust in His holy name.
May Your unfailing love rest upon us, O LORD, even as
we put our hope in You.

Psalm 33:21-22

We all need security. When difficult situations threaten to overwhelm us, most of us lean heavily on family and friends for help and support. But this prayer reminds us that, in the long run, only the Almighty God can protect and save us.

It is fitting to admit our dependence on the Lord when we come to Him in prayer. Remember that He is our Shield and Protector. As we focus on this wonderful truth, our fear will turn into praise.

Become quiet for a few minutes and think about the ways in which you seek security, in both big and small situations. Then confess to God that, in future, you will trust fully in Him alone.

*Lord Jesus, our hope and salvation surround us with
Your unfathomable love and protection. Amen.*

Praise for the Ways of God

Then my soul will rejoice in the LORD and delight
in His salvation. My whole being will exclaim,
"Who is like You, O LORD?"

Psalm 35:9-10

The splendor of all people fades in comparison with the mighty deeds of God. One day all people will bow before God in worship and declare His might and justice with loud cries. On this day all honor and glory will be given to Him.

But don't wait for that day. In your prayer time today, follow David's example and praise and thank God for saving you and allowing you to put your trust and hope in Him.

Loving Father, no one can compare with You. Therefore I will praise You as long as I live. Amen.

Praise for God's Power

The seas have lifted up their voice. Mightier than the thunder of the great waters, mightier than the breakers of the sea – the Lord on high is mighty.

Psalm 93:3-4

Through the ages people have marveled at the wonders of God's creation; especially the seas. The angry waves that break against the rocks and crash along the coast demonstrate the over-whelming power of water.

And yet, as powerful as the water is, the might of the God who created everything far surpasses all the powers of nature. Nothing in nature can be compared to the might of God.

If God's power is so much greater than the might of nature, He can undoubtedly handle any human problems. Don't allow desperate situations to undermine your trust in God. When you pray today, remember that God is mightier than the waters of the sea.

Creator God, we praise and glorify You because You are mightier than any created force in nature, and You put Your power at our disposal. Amen.

July 31

August

Comfort and Compassion

Comfort for the Future

Now the dwelling of God is with men, and He will live with them. They will be His people, and God Himself will be with them and be their God.

Revelation 21:3

Fear casts a very dark shadow over the future. But when you find refuge in the living Christ, you realize that regardless of how ominous things might appear, everything is still under God's control. The Lord God Almighty still reigns and has not abandoned His Creation.

To believe that God is working out His divine plan, in spite of man's sinfulness, enables you to maintain a well-balanced and calm attitude.

So, you can either look to the future without God and feel depressed and fearful, or you can believe in God's plan of redemption for mankind and approach the future with trust and confidence.

Eternal God, I believe that You are in control of this world. Therefore I can face the future with confidence and hope in Your salvation. Amen.

The Compassionate Christ

When He saw the crowds, He had compassion on them,
because they were harassed and helpless, like sheep
without a shepherd.

Matthew 9:36

Compassion is one of the outstanding characteristics of the unique personality of Jesus Christ.

The attitude that He revealed when talking to people not only stimulated their minds, but captured their hearts as well. They felt His love for them and responded by loving Him in return.

Because the immortal Christ is still alive, His compassion for humankind is just as real and true today as it was when He walked the dusty roads of Palestine. If you don't know where to turn for strength and inspiration, then remember the compassion of Jesus Christ. He is with you in all your distress and encourages you through the power of His love.

*Savior, may Your love and compassion inspire and
strengthen me today. Amen.*

August 2

Be a Comforter

They approach and come forward; each helps the other
and says to his brother, "Be strong!"

Isaiah 41:5-6

Life is not easy. But if you complain about your
fate and feel that God has let you down, you
only succeed in creating more misery and despair.

If the eternal Spirit of the living Christ lives in
you, He will prevent you from sinking into the
quicksand of despair. Cast your cares upon God.
After all, He knows about everything. Then you
will be able to live creatively and courageously.
Through the power of Christ's indwelling Spirit,
you can triumph over any negative circumstance.

*Powerful Savior, let my faith be so positive and
strong that I will be able to assist others
to overcome their despair. Amen.*

God Is a Father Who Cares

There you saw how the LORD your God carried you, as
a father carries his son, all the way you went until you
reached this place.

Deuteronomy 1:31

Life is seldom a smooth, problem-free road; times
of peace and calm alternate with frustration,
disappointments and setbacks.

If you yield to the temptation of being controlled by these feelings, your life will become
empty and aimless – robbed of its joy, purpose
and meaning.

Nobody escapes the disappointments of life,
but people who have faith in the promises of
God know that He is with them during the
hard times.

When a crisis occurs in your life, the wise
thing to do is to turn to God. "Cast all your
anxiety on Him, because He cares for you"
(1 Pet. 5:7).

*God, in times of crisis, I turn to You because
I know You love me and will help me,
no matter what I face. Amen.*

Comfort and Strength

May our Lord Jesus Christ Himself and God our Father, who loved us and by His grace gave us eternal encouragement and good hope, encourage your hearts and strengthen you in every good deed and word.

2 Thessalonians 2:16-17

When Paul wrote this letter to the church in Thessalonica, he was deeply concerned about the persecution they were bound to face.

Paul never sugar-coated true Christian discipleship. Above all, he wanted Christians to be willing to endure affliction for Christ's sake.

This prayer reveals a fatherly concern, prayed from his heart for the congregation because he could not always be with them. He prayed for God to comfort them and to give them strength. These special promises are meant for all God's children. We, too, can draw near to God and ask Him to comfort us and give us strength.

Lord Jesus, comfort our hearts and give us strength to do and say only what is right and true. Amen.

August 5

The Blessing of a Broken Heart

"Blessed are those who mourn,
for they will be comforted."

Matthew 5:4

If you are lost in sadness and sorrow, remember that your Great Comforter and Friend holds your hand firmly in His. You have a Mediator who died on the cross for you, rose from the dead, and ascended to heaven where He interceded for your comfort.

Christ never leaves you in your distress. He is with you in the fiery oven, in the stormy seas, and in the valley of the shadow of death.

Trust in Him who will not allow anything to happen to us that will harm us. God Himself said, "Blessed are those who mourn, for they will be comforted."

Jesus, Man of Sorrows, You drank Your cup of bitterness to the lees. Help me to do the same. Amen.

Comfort through Tears

Record my lament; list my tears on Your
scroll – are they not in Your record?

Psalm 56:8

Tears allow us to release our sorrow and grief
in a natural way. They are not a sign of weakness,
but arise from love, tenderness and compassion.
Tears alleviate our sorrow and hasten
the healing of our hearts. God is moved by our
grief and, through our tears, He provides us
with a way of dealing with sorrow.

When Jesus wept, God showed us the sanctity
of tears. He was powerful enough to remove
the cause of sorrow, yet human enough
to shed tears Himself.

Thank God for the healing, delivering and
purifying power of sincere tears. They soften
grief, bring acceptance and eventually lead to
joy.

*O Holy Comforter, I thank You that I can find comfort
and solace through my tears; that they make my grief
bearable and bring me closer to You. Amen.*

August 7

Share Your Burdens
with Christ

Cast all your anxiety on Him because He cares for you.

1 Peter 5:7

There are many aspects of life that can keep us up at night, but it is when we are facing these problems that we must trust God. Jesus promised never to abandon us. He even invites those who are weary and overburdened to come to Him for rest. He will never turn away anyone who comes to Him.

God does not necessarily offer you instant solutions, or make all your problems simply disappear because you pray. But if you place your faith and trust in God and confide in Him in prayer, He will enable you to think clearly and act positively. In His strength you will be able to handle your problems according to the will of God.

Soothe my restless heart, O Holy Spirit. Calm the tempestuous storms that rage. Lead me to quiet waters so that I can experience peace of mind. Amen.

He Carries Us Day by Day

Our God is a God who saves; from the Sovereign
LORD comes escape from death. Surely God
will crush the heads of His enemies.

Psalm 68:20-21

In the presence of God, meditate on the image that's presented in this passage. Place yourself in David's shoes. When you talk to God about your needs and concerns, imagine that God's arms are surrounding you with loving protection and allow His encompassing presence to comfort you.

What images do you have in your mind when you pray? Do you have a picture of a loving Father who hears the cries of His child? Or of a mighty warrior who has charge over countless legions of angels who are ready to do His bidding?

David's prayer provides an intimate image of God who carries His child in His loving arms.

Thank You, Lord, that You carry me to safety in Your eternal arms and that I am always safe with You. Amen.

August 9

The Compassionate Jesus

When He saw the crowds, He had compassion on them, because they were harassed and helpless, like sheep without a shepherd.

Matthew 9:36

Compassion is a distinctive characteristic of Jesus' personality. It flowed from the very center of His heart and filled His teachings. People enjoyed listening to Him and walked many miles just to hear Him. The brief record that we have of what He did and taught in three years reveals the depth of His wisdom and the uniqueness of His revelation of God the Father.

If life has disappointed you, or if you have failed and are filled with despair and have no idea where to turn to for inspiration and strength, remember the compassion of Jesus. In the power of His love He encourages you to persevere and to rebuild your life.

Compassionate Lord, thank You for
Your love that renews my life. Amen.

August 10

Christ Cares for You

Cast all your anxiety on Him because He cares for you.

1 Peter 5:7

At times the burdens of life seem overwhelming and all the blessings you've received seem to have vanished. It might sound very courageous to state that you can handle everything that life throws at you, but if your spirit is broken and your ability to recover has diminished, you need a real and vital relationship with God to help you get through.

The glorious truth is that your heavenly Father cares for you. He longs to share your life with you. Every burden and anxiety will be a new opportunity to grow in the presence of God.

*Holy Father, I am strengthened and inspired
when I consider the great sacrifice of love
that You made for me. Amen.*

August 11

Compassionate and Merciful Is the Lord

The LORD is compassionate and gracious,
slow to anger, abounding in love.

Psalm 103:8, 11-12

We often pray for our family, loved ones, friends and people in need, but some of our prayers need to be exclusively about God. That is what David did in Psalm 103; he praised the unequivocal love of God.

David praises God because He does not remain angry forever, and He does not punish us as we deserve. His love is as great as the span of the heavens above the earth. He removes our sins from us so that we do not need to dwell on them any longer.

David expresses His gratitude and admiration for God's greatness. Follow David's example and spend the next few minutes expressing gratitude to God in prayer.

Lord, our Lord, You are compassionate and merciful,
long-suffering and full of love. For that we
praise and thank You. Amen.

"Be Still, and Know that I am God"

The LORD said to Job: "Will the one who contends with the Almighty correct Him?" Then Job answered the LORD: "I am unworthy – how can I reply to You?"

Job 40:1-4

Job lost everything. He was left with a few friends who tried to understand what had happened to him, but they did not recognize God's eternal wisdom.

God does not need to give an explanation to any of us. His knowledge and might far surpass ours. We might never fully understand His ways, but we should know enough of His loving nature to be able to trust Him.

Bring your difficult questions to God, but be careful that they don't become an excuse to blame Him for your problems. God is righteous and His actions and thoughts are far above your understanding.

Righteous God, I do not always understand the things that happen, but I am content in the knowledge that You have all the answers. Amen.

A Prayer in Times
of Discouragement

My soul is weary with sorrow; strengthen me according
to Your word. Keep me from deceitful ways; be gracious
to me through Your law.

Psalm 119:28-29

To whom do you turn when you feel completely disheartened? Turn to the Word of God
and His commandments. There you will find
renewal. Even the psalmist who was weary
and "laid low in the dust" (Ps. 119:25) found
renewal in wanting to know more of God and
His ways.

In the secular and self-assured world we
live in, despair is fairly common. Even when
you feel most discouraged, seek God's help to
enable you to fully understand this truth: God
knows about our discouragement and despair
and He will handle every situation that comes
our way.

God of Comfort, I weep from sorrow and despair.
Encourage me through Your Word. Amen.

The Sound of Silence

After the fire came a gentle whisper.

1 Kings 19:12

To enjoy and appreciate silence is one of the small joys of life. It is then that your spirit becomes receptive to the presence of God.

Enter the silence with a prayer that the Holy Spirit will fill your thoughts with a Christian quality – it can be any aspect of His holy Being that appeals to you at that moment. When you are alone with God in silence and you become aware of His living presence, your time of quiet reflection becomes a time of spiritual empowerment and inspiration.

In God's presence you can gather strength for daily life with all of its demands and responsibilities.

Lord, I will wait upon You in quiet trust.
I know that You will disperse my doubts
and strengthen my faith anew. Amen.

God Wants to Be
Your Partner

*Devise your strategy, but it will be thwarted; propose
your plan, but it will not stand, for God is with us.*

Isaiah 8:10

Many of us view certain circumstances with trepidation and fear. The only safe way to venture on life's journey with any certainty is to do so in partnership with God. He created the world and everything in it – including you, and He will not allow His Creation to be overpowered.

In order for you to conquer your fears and anxieties amidst threats and adversities, it is essential for you to have an intimate relationship with the living Christ. You must be one in spirit with Him so that, through the Holy Spirit, He can work in and through you. Then you will be able to face every challenge and danger in God's ever-victorious name.

*Thank You, Lord, that You clothe me in armor so that
I may remain standing in this world. You deliver me
from evil and lead me to victory. Amen.*

God As Your Guide

Is anyone of you in trouble? He should pray.
Is anyone happy? Let him sing songs of praise.

James 5:13

When you confront a problem in life, you must never forget to go to the One who mercifully offered to be your Father, with your distress, anxiety and confusion.

Find consolation and strength in Jesus Christ because He cares for you and He fully understands your distress and anxiety. Go to the throne of mercy and lay your problems before Him. Give yourself fully to Him in serious prayer and supplication. Then experience the serenity and peace of mind that only He can give you.

Thank God that He lays His hands on you, guiding you safely through the labyrinth of life.

God, You are the only true Comforter. Thank You for inspiring me and strengthening me time after time. You are my refuge and my shelter. Amen.

August 17

Do God's Work

Never tire of doing what is right.

2 Thessalonians 3:13

How often have you met people who feel that there is little or no sense in trying to do the right thing, or to live a life caring about other people?

Regardless of how justified you might feel in adopting this attitude, it will only lead to self-centeredness and a feeling of complacency.

It also clashes directly with the doctrines of Jesus Christ. In spite of the thankless disposition of people, He gave His all to mankind and never gave up on us.

In today's world it is not easy to display the attitude of Jesus. However, you must remember that what you do for other people, you also do for the Master.

Lord, please strengthen us. Give us a steady hand in order to never cease doing Your work. Amen.

You Are Special to God

For God does not show favoritism.

Romans 2:11

God has no "favorites". Whether you are an ordinary person, or a celebrity, in God's eyes you are special because you are one of His creatures; His child and He loves you. You are a unique creation of His hand and you have special value in His eyes.

So many people torture themselves with the thought that they are unworthy in comparison to other believers, or that they have disappointed God. But Jesus reached out to both the worthy and the unworthy. They all received His love, care, grace and compassion.

Do not give in to feelings of inferiority or unworthiness. The Redeemer came for the salvation of all people; both the righteous and sinners.

I know that You live and that You have forgiven my sins. Through Your precious blood I have inherited peace. Amen.

God Is Always with You

For men are not cast off by the Lord forever. Though He brings grief, He will show compassion.

Lamentations 3:31-32

There are some people who believe that they are totally alone in this world. They feel that they have no one to turn to for help and comfort in times of trouble.

Although it is true that some people do not enjoy the warmth of a family life, or the company of intimate friends, it does not mean that they are alone. God is always with us. He even says, "Surely I am with you always, to the very end of the age" (Matt. 28:20).

So if you feel all alone, turn to Jesus this very moment and remember that He will never leave you nor forsake you.

You are so patient, Lord. You will never forsake man in his feebleness, but You will always be by our side in compassion. Thank You for Your presence. Amen.

When the Past Haunts You

One thing I do: Forgetting what is behind and straining toward what is ahead.

Philippians 3:13

If you are haunted by thoughts about "what could have been", you cannot experience the freedom of spirit that is your spiritual heritage. Perhaps a foolish decision or misguided action robbed your life of peace and joy.

Through the merciful atonement of Christ, you see a vision of what you can become in Him. The past might stir burning shame in your heart, but the shining halo of the future supersedes the dismal gloom of the past.

When you choose a new life in Jesus, you look ahead to a sparkling future, where you start every day anew with God – undisturbed by negative thoughts about failures and flaws of the past.

We cannot cease praising You for Your miraculous works of redemption. Through Your mercy, even Your weakest child is redeemed. Amen.

August 21

Find Strength and Comfort in the Word

Open my eyes that I may see
wonderful things in Your law.

Psalm 119:18

Disillusion and dejection are very common today, giving people a melancholy and gloomy outlook on life.

In order for you to live and not merely exist, it is essential to have a positive attitude towards life. When everything goes well, enjoy life and praise God. But when things do not go that well, you need a strong faith to overcome the stumbling blocks and step out triumphantly.

To prevent falling prey to discouragement and pessimism in such times, search the Scriptures for testimony of the work of the Almighty God. You will find many examples of ordinary people who overcame hostile forces in the name of the Lord.

You reveal Yourself in Your Word. It is trustworthy, steadfast and unfailing. Thank You that I may know this Word contains life. Amen.

A Caring Heart (1)

"Blessed are the merciful, for they will be shown mercy."

Matthew 5:7

Mercy is to personally care about another's distress and to show understanding for the circumstances of others. In the parable Jesus tells in Luke, He describes three types of people: Takers, Hoarders and Givers.

The highwaymen are the Takers. Their philosophy is: "Everything that is yours, is mine. I'll take it." They rob the innocent traveler and walk away from the scene. These people are not necessarily your enemies, sometimes they are even your friends who take everything that they can from you and then leave you to your fate.

Takers are only interested in what they can obtain for their own selfish purposes. They have yet to understand what mercy is all about.

Lord Jesus, give me a caring heart such as You had for sinners, prostitutes and outcasts, so that I can do Your work in this world. Amen.

A Caring Heart (2)

"Blessed are the merciful, for they will be shown mercy."

Matthew 5:7

When a priest and a Levite came along the road and saw a man lying there, they moved to the other side. These are the Hoarders in life whose philosophy is, "Everything that is mine, is mine. I'll keep it." They are people with callous hearts, who gather only for themselves.

Then a Samaritan came upon the wounded man and felt deeply sorry for him. He represents the Givers in life – people who practice mercy and display Christian love. Their philosophy is, "Everything that is mine, is yours. I'll give it." The Samaritan gave of his money, possessions, time, sympathy and comfort without even asking whether it was deserved.

When we show mercy to others, God will have mercy on us.

Lord Jesus, thank You for having mercy on me
when I did not deserve it. Help me to do
the same for my fellow man. Amen.

August 24

A Temple of God

For this God is our God for ever and ever; He will be our guide even to the end.

Psalm 48:14

This psalm of the Sons of Korah is about the temple and the God of the temple. The God of the temple is more important than the temple itself – this must be true of us as well.

Our religion should point to God, and not to the structures that we erect around our religion. We must worship the Lord in such a way that people notice Him rather than beautiful clothes, expensive buildings and lofty prayers.

Then our lives will have the quality of Jerusalem, the city that points to God and displays the glory of God.

Eternal and unchanging God, thank You that You are also my God and that You will guide me safely into the house of the Father. Amen.

August 25

Who Am I?

Yet to all who received Him, to those who believed in His name, He gave the right to become children of God.

John 1:12

In all of our lives there are days when everything looks dismal. In times of dejection and depression, it is not uncommon for people to question their identity and the purpose of life.

If you find yourself doing this, remember the glorious heritage that you have received through the grace of God. Through your faith in Jesus Christ, and by embracing Him as your Savior, your life will find new meaning and purpose because you no longer have to search for your identity. You identify with the living Christ and become a child of God. Life can have no greater meaning than that.

God of grace and love, help me when life is at its lowest ebb to put my hope and faith in You and to cherish the truth in my heart that I am a child of God! Amen.

August 26

Be a Comforter

They approach and come forward; each helps the other
and says to his brother, "Be strong!"

Isaiah 41:5-6

Life is not easy, and there are many factors that contribute to a difficult life.

As a Christian, you are not necessarily free from temptations and problems. However, the difference lies in your approach to these things. Don't just join the choir of moans – that will only create more misery and despair.

If you have the Holy Spirit of the living Christ in you, He will prevent you from sinking into the quicksand of a depressed and negative attitude. You will look for solutions to life's problems, and if the answers escape you, you will be content, in childlike faith, to cast your cares upon Christ. After all, God knows everything about everything and He has a glorious future planned for you.

Lord, help me to remember that You have a wonderful
plan for my life. Let me take comfort in that. Amen.

Are You Uninvolved?

Then the LORD said to Cain, "Where is your
brother Abel?" "I don't know," he replied.
"Am I my brother's keeper?"

Genesis 4:9

Much of the evil in the world can be ascribed to
a lack of involvement in the face of the distress
of our fellow man.

Unfortunately there are many people who,
for a variety of reasons, are inclined to follow
the example of the priest and the Levite in the
parable of the Good Samaritan and "pass on
the other side" instead of feeling sorry for the
victim.

Jesus gave us two commandments that He
emphasized as the most important. Love God
with your entire being, and love your neighbor
as yourself. There is no place in the Christian
faith for ignoring your fellow man. Your concern for the well-being of others is a barometer
of your love for God.

Use me, Lord, to serve amongst my fellow man. Amen.

August 28

Caring for Others
Could Cure the World

Each of you should look not only to your own interests, but also to the interests of others.

Philippians 2:4

Jesus Christ devoted His whole life to caring for others. His love for people was all embracing. This was obvious in His relationship with everyone He came across. Despite the circumstances, or regardless of them, His first thought was always for others – even when He was nailed to the cross.

Jesus commanded His followers to love one another as He loves us. It is unavoidable that this will include self-sacrifice. In our ministry of love to one another, we must show the same compassion and forgiving love that the Master has for us. Only in doing so can the wounds of this world be healed.

Holy Spirit of God, fill me with the desire and ability to love my neighbor as You love me. Amen.

Be Strong!

Say to those with fearful hearts, "Be strong,
do not fear; your God will come."

Isaiah 35:4

We all experience discouragement at some point in our lives. If you feel that your dreams have been shattered and your efforts have come to nothing, do not allow self-pity to sow the seed of discouragement in your spirit.

There are spiritual reserves from which you can draw that will give you hope and a sense of purpose. Do not rely on your own sources of inspiration, because when these fail you will lose your vision and become discouraged.

God is your constant source of inspiration. Remember, you do not fight alone against negative feelings and emotions. God is on your side and He is waiting to pick you up so that you may proceed with joy and be ultimately triumphant.

I thank You heavenly Father, that through the power of Your residing Spirit, I can triumph over discouragement. Amen.

August 30

Run to Jesus

When He saw the crowds, He had compassion on them, because they were harassed and helpless, like sheep without a shepherd.

Matthew 9:36

Jesus' compassion was a sign of His greatness, not an indication of weakness. It resided in the center of His heart and His teachings.

Scripture informs us that ordinary people liked to listen to Jesus and that they took long journeys to hear Him. What Jesus told the people revealed how close He was to the Father and how compassionate He was.

If you are feeling overwhelmed by life and full of despair, remember Jesus and His loving compassion. Run to His open arms and allow Him to soothe and comfort you.

Compassionate Master, let Your love renew my life so that I may rejoice in Your love. Amen.

September

God's Loving Protection

Divine Protection

They remembered that God was their Rock, that God
most High was their Redeemer.

Psalm 78:35

Many times in the history of the world it seemed as if all was lost and all hope was gone.

Yet God has saved people and nations from devastation in miraculous ways, and has enabled them to overcome dangers and transform defeat into glorious victory.

These cases should serve as a constant reminder of the victorious omnipotence of God in all spheres of life. No circumstances are too small or too big for Him, and no prayer will remain unheard or unanswered. Only in Him will you find deliverance from your distress.

*Lord my God, You are a safe fortress to me, a
shield against every calamity that threatens to overwhelm me. Knowing this, I step with confidence
into the unknown. Amen.*

Omnipotent Protector

The Lord is my rock, my fortress and my deliverer; my
God is my rock, in whom I take refuge.

2 Samuel 22:2-3

When we are afflicted and needy, the love and
omnipotence of God protects us. We can overcome any challenge, adversity or problem if
we only steadfastly trust in His loving care and
grace.

He will command His angels to watch over
us and protect us from any danger. We will not
be overwhelmed by evil and left powerless.
The ability He gives us to choose between what
is good and right and what is wrong, will help
us to act wisely.

Through the love that is in our hearts, we
give and receive love. Then peace and joy fill
our minds and hearts, and we are assured that
we have an omnipotent Protector.

*Father, I bow before You in grateful humility because
You have given me Your light and Your wisdom so
that I can always do what is right. Amen.*

September 2

God Remains in Control

He is before all things, and in Him
all things hold together.

Colossians 1:17

Sometimes it seems as if everything is going wrong. Before giving in to despondency, however, acknowledge the greatness, glory and constancy of God. He called the world into existence; He created humankind; He has kept vigil over His Creation, cared for us through the ages and sheltered us in every disaster. He is the Creator God who will never abandon His workmanship. In His vast love He gave His Son to this world, so that whoever believes in Him shall not perish but have everlasting life (see John 3:16).

Therefore hold on to His promises; place your trust and faith in the living Christ, and through Him you will survive all danger and adversity.

You are eternal, Lord, and the workmanship of Your Creation bears testimony to Your great glory. The universe celebrates Your great name. Amen.

September 3

The Reassuring Love of God

> I love the LORD, for He heard my voice;
> He heard my cry for mercy.
>
> Psalm 116:1

There comes a time in each of our lives when we urgently need reassurance for peace of mind and to calm our spirit.

Regardless of how self-assured you may be, there will come a time in your life when you will recognize that you have such a need. But what if there is no one to assist you in your crucial time? What are you supposed to do then?

The answer lies in today's Scripture verse. God is always there as a refuge and help in time of need. He is always there when you need Him, He always hears when you call to Him from the depths and you can be assured that He will answer your prayers.

O Lord, my God, I love You with all my heart and know that all things happen for my good because You love me. Amen.

I Am with You!

"When you pass through the waters, I will be with you; and when you pass through the rivers, they will not sweep over you. When you walk through the fire, you will not be burned; the flames will not set you ablaze."

Isaiah 43:2

It requires great faith and a strong character to be able to work through adversity and disappointment. Many seemingly strong people eventually collapse under their burdens.

The Lord never promised that our lives would be trouble-free just because we choose to serve Him. But He did promise to be there for us at all times, and help us over life's hurdles. Knowing that you don't have to tackle the afflictions of life on your own is a comforting and reassuring thought.

When problems mar your view and place pressure on you, turn to Christ. He is your heavenly Companion. Overcome your problems in the peace of His presence.

Thank You, omnipotent Father, that I can say with confidence that You are with me day by day. Amen.

A Safe Haven

The LORD is my rock and my fortress and my deliverer;
my God, my strength, in whom I will trust;
my shield and the horn of my salvation.

Psalm 18:2 (NKJV)

We all seek shelter at one time or another. It may be in the security of your home, or a shelter against the wind and rain.

Our spiritual and intellectual faculties are also often ravaged by the storms of life. We all need a safe and secure haven where we can find shelter from these storms and be protected from devastating emotional consequences.

Even when it seems as if everything is lost, entrust yourself to the love of Jesus Christ. However dark the road ahead may seem, Christ, in His love, is your shelter and safe haven.

Thank You, my God, that I find shelter in You and that I will be safe now and for all eternity. Amen.

September 6

God Is a Refuge

Is any one of you in trouble? He should pray. Is anyone happy? Let him sing songs of praise.

James 5:13

When we face a crisis, prayer is sadly only used as a last desperate act when all other efforts have failed.

Even though we are encouraged to call on God throughout Scripture, the average person looks for human solutions first, rather than considering God's loving invitation. Over and over He promises His assistance and grace to those who call on Him in their time of need.

Regardless of what the crisis in your life may be, lay your problem before Him in trust and He will transform your crisis into a blessing.

Father, I am experiencing a crisis. Give me Your peace so that I can see things from Your perspective and make the right decisions. Amen.

Your Anchor in Life

"There is no one holy like the LORD; there is no
one besides You; there is no Rock like our God."

1 Samuel 2:2

When faced with problems, some people turn
to professional counselors for advice, medical
assistance or friends, while others try to fight
their way through the dilemma in their own
strength.

While all these methods can provide some
help, they can't provide assurance that the
problem won't occur again, or that the person
will be able to handle it if it does. The only sure
and lasting solution comes from God.

Never make the mistake of leaving God out
of your life. Other things can help you survive,
but only God can give you abiding peace.

*Savior, by putting my life in Your hands I know that
all things work together for my benefit because You
love me. Amen.*

A God Who Encourages

May the God who gives endurance and
encouragement give you a spirit of unity among
yourselves as you follow Christ Jesus.

Romans 15:5

If you reach the point in life where you feel
discouraged and unable to cope, it is good to
spend quality time in the presence of God.
There you will receive the encouragement that
only He can give.

Be still and surrender yourself anew to Him,
and remember that He is God. In the silence of
His divine presence, you can recall all His glorious promises of encouragement. Remember
that in both the storm and the stillness, God is
with you. He does not want you to remain in
the dark valley of despondency; He will give
you the strength to complete the task He has
set before you.

*Holy God, when life is too much for me, I withdraw
into Your presence and there I find the comfort and the
strength that I need. Amen.*

Feeling Discouraged?

Say to those with fearful hearts, "Be strong,
do not fear; your God will come."

Isaiah 35:4

We all feel discouraged sometimes. It manifests itself in different ways, but always leaves you disillusioned, wondering whether all your efforts were worth the trouble. Only those who strive for a goal can be discouraged.

Ask God to help you. He wants to see you overcome the effects of discouragement and move forward towards your goal. You do not fight alone against discouragement. God is on your side and He is ready to lift you up so that you can continue with joy.

*I thank You, heavenly Father, that through the power
of Your Holy Spirit I can triumph over any
discouragement. Amen.*

September 10

Blessed Assurance

He will never leave you nor forsake you.

Deuteronomy 31:6

When Joshua was appointed as Moses' successor, he received the blessed assurance that God would never leave him nor forsake him. Joshua led the people of Israel into the Promised Land with the promise that God would be by his side no matter what.

Are you tired, troubled or confused? Does the road ahead seem strewn with problems, concerns and troubles? Ask the Lord to help you and you will discover the truth of Deuteronomy 31:6. He will grant you peace and joy in abundance. If you ask Him, you will find that the Lord is as faithful as He promised in His Word.

Father God, thank You that I have the assurance that You will never fail me nor forsake me. Forgive me for the times when I failed and disappointed You. Amen.

September 11

God Hears My Cry

I call to the LORD, who is worthy of praise,
and I am saved from my enemies.

2 Samuel 22:4

There is no greater feeling than arriving home safely after a dangerous journey. We like to tell others about our adventures, but we often forget to worship God with prayers of praise for granting us safe passage.

When God delivers us out of desperate situations, we should remember to come quietly before Him for a while and thank Him for what He has done.

How many evils does God protect us from daily? How often have we felt His loving protection over our lives and our loved ones? How can we then forget to thank Him in prayerful worship?

*I worship You, Lord my God, because You have saved
me from so much evil. Amen.*

From Where Does My Help Come?

I lift up my eyes to the hills – where does my help come from? My help comes from the Lord, the Maker of heaven and earth. He will not let your foot slip – He who watches over you will not slumber.

Psalm 121:1-3

The role of security guards is to protect a building from intruders. If guards do not pay attention to their surroundings, then intruders can easily slip in unnoticed.

The Lord never loses concentration while He watches over you. He watches over you constantly to make sure that you do not stumble or fall. Our God never loses focus and will be our protective covering day in and day out.

The one who prays knows that God will protect him because God, who made the heavens and the earth, who neither slumbers nor sleeps, is able to protect His children perfectly at all times.

I thank You, Almighty God, that You watch over me day and night and keep me safe from all danger. Amen.

Trust in the Lord Forever

You will keep in perfect peace him whose mind is steadfast, because he trusts in You. Trust in the LORD forever,
for the LORD, the LORD, is the Rock eternal.

Isaiah 26:3-4

We all want to feel safe from the attack of enemies and strangers. In this prayer of praise
from Isaiah, believers declare that their safety
is in the Lord.

In biblical times, in Israel, safety meant being able to live in a city with strong walls that
would keep the enemy out. However, walls of
stone can collapse, but our God will be able to
protect and guard the righteous forever. Therefore believers need never fear anyone!

Allow this Scripture passage to encourage
you to focus your thoughts on the Almighty
God. Reaffirm your trust in Him today and experience the peace that this kind of trust can
bring.

*Sovereign God, help me to focus my thoughts on You
and to trust You at all times, because You are my
protector and my eternal Rock. Amen.*

September 14

Our Hiding Place

The LORD is a refuge for the oppressed, a stronghold in
times of trouble. Those who know Your name will
trust in You, for You, LORD, have never
forsaken those who seek You.

Psalm 9:9-10

David went through intense suffering in his life.
He was a fugitive from King Saul, the mightiest
man in the land, and on one occasion even his
own son turned against him.

Therefore, when David praised God for being a refuge for people in danger, he was not
talking in hypothetical or abstract terms. Placing his trust in God was a matter of life or death
for him. And God never let him down.

In times of trial and tribulation, remember
that God always watches over you. He will
never forsake those who call upon Him, nor let
them down.

*Thank You, mighty God, that we can find a safe refuge
in You and that we can hide in You. Thank You that
You never turn away those who come to You. Amen.*

September 15

My Help Comes from the Lord

O LORD, how many are my foes! How many rise up against me! Many are saying of me, "God will not deliver him." But You are a shield around me. I lie down and sleep; I wake again, because the LORD sustains me.

Psalm 3:1-3, 5

If enemies are pursuing you and trying to make you doubt the power of God's deliverance by saying, "God will not deliver you," then do what David did – call on God, who is your shield and protection. If you do this, then you will be able to lie down and sleep in peace, because God will watch over you.

There is no need to ever be afraid because God is our protector. He always looks after His children; He will never stop looking after us.

Lord, my loving God, I know that You watch over me because You are my shield and protection. Amen.

Your Love, O Lord, Endures Forever

Though I walk in the midst of trouble, You preserve my life; You stretch out Your hand against the anger of my foes, with Your right hand You save me. The LORD will fulfill His purpose for me; do not abandon the works of Your hands.

Psalm 138:7-8

Sometimes you might face a situation where it seems as if God has abandoned you when you need Him most, but if you have faith, you know that that is not true.

"The LORD will fulfill His purpose for me." Cling to this truth in times of trial and trouble because you know that the Lord will never neglect His children – the works of His hands.

In your prayer time today, thank God for the good plan that He has for your life. In those dark moments when it seems as if He has forsaken you, remember that God is faithful and you can never drift away from His love.

Loving God, protect me from the anger of my enemies. Thank You that there is no end to Your love. Amen.

God Is My Refuge

Your word is a lamp to my feet and a light for my path.

Psalm 119:105

In this Scripture verse, the lamp symbolizes the guidance, wisdom and knowledge that we find in the Word. This life is like a dark wilderness through which we must find a way and, just as a lamp helps a traveler in the dark, the Word is a light on our path so we will not stumble.

Pray for light and truth from God's Word so that you can stay on the path of life. Ask God to guide you through the situations that could become stumbling blocks on your spiritual path and commit yourself anew to Him and His Word today.

Thank You, merciful God, that You light up our dark path with the light of Your Word. Help us to use Your light each day. Amen.

Let Your Hand Rest on Your People

Revive us, and we will call on Your name. Restore us,
O Lord God Almighty; make Your face shine upon us,
that we may be saved.

Psalm 80:18-19

When you come to the end of your own reserves and find yourself worn out, there is only one place to which you can flee for refuge. God is your only hope for strength.

God created you to fellowship with Him; He wants you to call on His name. You are the branches of His vine and therefore you are completely dependent on the One who planted you – God Himself.

Thank God for the refuge He offers you and for the love that He showers on you. And when you feel that you cannot go any further, ask Him once again to renew your strength for the road that you must follow.

Provider God, let Your holy countenance shine down on us in love and provide our basic needs. Amen.

Stay Close to the Shepherd

Even when I walk through the darkest valley, I will
not be afraid, for you are close beside me. Your
rod and Your staff protect and comfort me.

Psalm 23:4 (NLT)

Scripture never tries to hide the dark shadows
of life – not even death. This Scripture verse describes how God is always with us, even in the
valley of the shadow of death. Therefore we
should fear no evil because God is with us.

From time to time we should recall the moments in our lives where God was with us in
the valley. Stay close to Him because He will
always be with us, through the rest of the year
and for the rest of our lives, because He promised to never leave us.

*Omnipresent God, even when I walk through the
valley of the shadow of death, I will not fear, because I
know that You are always close to me. Amen.*

Rest in God's Care

Show the wonder of Your great love, You who save by Your right hand those who take refuge in You from their foes. Keep me as the apple of Your eye; hide me in the shadow of Your wings.

Psalm 17:7-8

You are the apple of the Lord's eye. God will protect you because He will answer your cries of distress; he is bending down, compassionate and interested in your prayer.

Believe in your heart that God will use His power to protect you. When you look to God with expectation, you receive the protection you so desperately seek.

Let this Scripture verse remind you that God is willing and able to protect you faithfully. He is the only One who can truly shield and protect you, so lay your cares at His feet.

I thank You, Almighty God, that You protect me as the apple of Your eye. Hide me in the shadow of Your wings. Amen.

September 21

Seek Shelter with God

My eyes are fixed on You, O Sovereign Lord; in You I take refuge – do not give me over to death. Keep me from the snares they have laid for me.

Psalm 141:8-9

A newspaper carried a report about a hiker who got lost and walked through a blinding snowstorm for hours without seeing any sign of life. Exhausted, hungry and almost freezing to death, he was ready to give up hope when he spotted a cabin between the trees.

How welcoming the sight of that cabin must have seemed to the hiker – his refuge and safe fortress. It literally saved his life.

Jesus represents that cabin for us – He is our refuge against the dangers surrounding us. Therefore it is comforting to know that when enemies surround us, we can call on God to deliver us. Cast all your cares and concerns onto God, He is your refuge and safe fortress.

Savior and Redeemer, today I look to You for help. Please open Your hand and provide in all my needs. Amen.

September 22

Secure in God

In the beginning You laid the foundations of the earth,
and the heavens are the work of Your hands. They
will perish, but You remain; they will all wear out
like a garment. But You remain the same,
and Your years will never end.

Psalm 102:25-27

Are you going through a time of great affliction and misery? Allow the words of this Scripture verse to soothe your worried soul and provide a ray of hope in your desperate situation.

Remember, you are a child of God. This God rises above all our problems, as well as above time and space. He is willing and able to keep His children safe and to let them live in His holy presence forever.

Should you find yourself in distress today because of the problems of life, then let God know of your anxieties and thank Him for providing stability in your ever-changing world.

O God, my refuge and my fortress, thank You for the security that You bring into my life. Amen.

Take Refuge in God

I will sing of Your strength, in the morning I will sing of Your love; for You are my fortress, my refuge in times of trouble. O my Strength, I sing praise to You; You, O God, are my fortress, my loving God.

Psalm 59:16-17

Love between people can be a source of great joy or of great pain – especially if someone's love is fickle and unpredictable. However, with God as your Savior, you need never feel that His love is fickle. In contrast to human love, God's love is infallible!

Because of this you can count on God to always be your refuge in times of trouble. When you experience difficult times, find your power, strength and refuge in the infallible love of God. It will never fail you.

Holy God, I seek Your shelter in times of difficulty and affliction. As I turn to You, let me experience Your infallible love. Amen.

When Dark Clouds Gather

Surely God is my salvation; I will trust and not be afraid. The LORD, the LORD is my strength and my song; He has become my salvation.

Isaiah 12:2

It would be extremely naïve to think that ominous clouds will never gather to darken our lives. It would be even more futile to try and ignore them, hoping they will just disappear, because the storm usually erupts – whether you want it to or not.

With God at the center of your life, however, you will be able to maintain balance at all times. The ominous clouds might still be present, but you will always see the silver lining, and you will have the steadfast knowledge that, behind every cloud, there is a loving Father who is still carving the holy design of your life because He loves you with a divine love.

Even when everything around me is shrouded in darkness, You will shield me. Thank You for supporting and shielding me through Your love – even though I do not deserve it. Amen.

When Things Go Wrong

Do not be afraid or discouraged because of this vast army. For the battle is not yours, but God's.

2 Chronicles 20:15

Sometimes you may feel that there is no reason for you to continue fighting the battle. You feel defeated and want to give up.

When these feelings get the better of you, you have probably ignored God. Overwhelmed by the forces against you, you have allowed the influence of evil to affect you negatively. By displaying such an attitude, you have subconsciously acknowledged that these destructive forces have greater control over your life than the omnipotence of your heavenly Father.

Hold on to the timeless truth, to your loyalty to God, and to everything He represents. Choose to join forces with the dynamic power of justice, and then no negative or destructive force can stand against you.

Lord, help me to count my blessings during crises. You will never abandon me. Even in difficult times I can count on Your blessings. Amen.

September 26

Our Loving Protector

For the eyes of the LORD range throughout the
earth to strengthen those whose hearts
are fully committed to Him.

2 Chronicles 16:9

Let us never think that we have drifted out of
the sphere of God's love. We read in His Word
that His eyes range throughout the earth in order to help those who put their trust in Him.
The Lord always knows who places their expectations in Him: He shelters them in times
of danger, helps them handle temptations and
problems, and comforts them in their sorrow.

What a blessed privilege it is to have such
a God as our protector. Wherever we find ourselves while living within His will, we can rest
assured that His eyes keep a loving watch over
us and that He is ready to hear when we call
and to help when we need Him.

*We praise Your great name, God, because You never
forsake those who trust in You. Amen.*

Dealing with Adversity

"Do not be distressed and do not be angry with yourselves for selling me here, because it was to save lives that God sent me ahead of you."

Genesis 45:5

There must have been many times in his life when Joseph felt that God had forsaken him. But after many years, when he became a prince in Egypt, he could say with conviction that God had been working positively in his life the whole time.

Being a child of God doesn't mean that you will not be subject to the same trials and tribulations as unbelievers.

Yet, when you are aware of the fact that God is your Father, you will realize that He turns problems to your advantage. God sees the pattern of your life in its entirety and He will achieve His perfect objective with it.

You are my only shelter, Lord, and I am helpless before You. You deliver me from evil and guide me when I am surrounded by darkness and have no hope. Amen.

September 28

God Performs His Wonders through You

Cast all your anxiety on Him because He cares for you.

1 Peter 5:7

Sometimes worries beyond your control prey on your mind; you may be concerned about your job, or an increase in rent. If you are anxious and worried about a personal matter, you must remember that God is greater than all the circumstances and situations that could befall you.

For a moment you may have allowed fear and uncertainty about the future to obscure your image of God. However, He is forever constant and He desires to share the deepest experience of your life with you. God's omnipotence will sweep away all petty thoughts and all uncertainty will disappear.

Your works are perfect, Lord, and even when I drink from the cup of bitterness; You will never forsake me but will help me to understand that, with You, I will survive. Amen.

God Hears Your Cry

I call on the LORD in my distress, and He answers me.

Psalm 120:1

It is essential for you to realize that you are never completely alone and that you are not without friends in this harsh world. Jesus, the living Christ, has promised to never leave nor forsake you. He offers you His friendship and all that He asks from you is to be obedient to His commandment of love.

Secure in this knowledge, you have the assurance of His constant presence in your life. He has already heard your call of distress and answered your prayer.

You know our deepest sorrow and hear our sighs. Help us, Lord, never to forget that You alone are our salvation and support. Amen.

September 30

October

Praise and Thanksgiving

Praise God!

My heart is steadfast, O God; I will sing and
make music with all my soul.

Psalm 108:1-2

We pray to thank God for what He has done for us, to lay our needs before Him, and to confess our sins to Him, but we often neglect to praise Him in our prayers.

Never underestimate the power of praise in your life. If someone impresses you, you praise him or her, so why shouldn't you shower God with your praise? He is indeed worthy of our love and thanksgiving.

If you focus on praising and glorifying God, you will create a very special relationship with the living Christ. Your prayer life will be transformed and your love for Him intensified. Through your praise you will become a stronger witness for Him.

Great and wonderful God, we want to exalt Your name and glorify You for all the wonders of Your love and grace that You give to us. Amen.

True Praise
and Thanksgiving

Heal me, O Lord, and I will be healed; save me and I
will be saved, for You are the one I praise.

Jeremiah 17:14

In Psalm 47 the psalmist appeals to all people to, "Clap your hands, all you nations; shout to God with cries of joy." It is impossible to clap your hands and sing exultantly to the glory of God and still remain gloomy. Praise is a powerful stimulant, so if you are feeling downhearted then start praising and thanking God now.

True praise and thanksgiving to God should not depend on your feelings. It is precisely when you are feeling depressed that you most need to praise Him. When you do, you will experience the wonderful, uplifting power of praise and you will be able to overcome any negative feelings that afflict you.

I want to lift my heart and my mind to You and exalt in Your goodness and greatness always. Amen.

The Blessing of a Grateful Heart

"He who sacrifices thank offerings honors Me."

Psalm 50:23

Sometimes a complaint is valid, but the danger of complaining is that it can become a habit. Eventually you forget that there are more things to be grateful for than to complain about. If you are complaining more often than you are expressing gratitude, then you are living an inferior quality of life.

Never let a day go by without consciously expressing your gratitude. Open your eyes to that which is beautiful around you and praise God for what you see and experience. When you start thanking God for His gifts of grace, He is already planning the next blessing for you.

Praise the Lord, O my soul, all my inmost being praise His holy name. Amen.

Giving Thanks

Sing and make music in your heart to the LORD, always
giving thanks to God the Father for everything, in the
name of our Lord Jesus Christ.

Ephesians 5:20

Many Christians have lost the art of giving
thanks. They are so overwhelmed by problems
that a cloud of depression has descended upon
them and they see very little to thank God for.

When a Christian stops giving thanks, he has
lost a source of great inspiration and spiritual
strength. Thanksgiving is a powerful force in
your spiritual life. It can dispel the dark clouds
of depression and despair.

To release the power of thanksgiving, start
each day with a sincere prayer of appreciation to God for the gift of life. You will discover that, by doing this, you will establish an
atmosphere for the day that will cause you to
live in victory.

*Holy Lord Jesus, I praise You because of Your great
love for me. Thank You for the gift of abundant and
eternal life that You give to me. Amen.*

The Blessing of Gratitude

Give thanks to the LORD, call on His name; make known among the nations what He has done.

1 Chronicles 16:8

In the hustle and bustle of everyday life it is easy to forget about ordinary courtesy. The habit of saying "Thank you" enriches every aspect of our lives. Always be ready to express thanks. You will soon discover how much joy you can bring to others. Apart from the fact that you enrich and bless the lives of others, your own life will be enriched. Never underestimate the power of gratitude.

All that we have, our heavenly Father has given to us. How much more will our lives be enriched if we learn to express gratitude toward Him?

Grant me a grateful heart, O God, for all the wondrous things that You have done for us, but above all, for the birth of Jesus, our Savior. Amen.

October 5

Shower God with Praise

My heart is steadfast, O God; I will sing and
make music with all my soul. Awake, harp
and lyre! I will awaken the dawn.

Psalm 108:1-2

Take a moment today to shower God with
praise. Think about all the remarkable things
He has done. Think of the miracles that flow
from Him and the extraordinary extent of His
love. Ponder for a moment the wonders of
the universe and Creation; of human life and
achievement.

Praise and glorify our benevolent God. He
is most worthy to receive our love and thanksgiving.

*Great and wonderful God, we want to exalt Your
name. We praise and glorify You for all the wonders of
Your love and grace that You give to us. Amen.*

Rejoice in the Lord!

Then the people of Israel – the priests, the Levites and the rest of the exiles – celebrated the dedication of the house of God with joy.

Ezra 6:16

Many Christians see Christianity as somber and attend church simply out of a false sense of duty. Such an attitude tragically deprives them of the greatest of all joys: joy in the Lord.

God offers you fullness of life. Turn to Him and you will become more aware of His life-giving Spirit. As you open yourself up to the Holy Spirit, you will find that your worship, Bible study and prayer life gain new meaning. If you place your trust in the living Christ, you will discover that God is no longer a remote being, but an integral part of your life.

Worship ought to be a joyful experience. Open yourself to the Holy Spirit and He will raise you from despondency to ecstasy in Christ.

*O Holy Spirit, come into my life and fill
me with the joy of the Lord. Amen.*

Be Continually Grateful

Continue to live in Him, rooted and built up in Him, strengthened in the faith as you were taught, and over-flowing with thankfulness.

Colossians 2:6-7

Many people tend to focus so much on the flaws around them that they fail to see the wonders of God and His grace.

God knows every detail of your life, from the cradle to the grave. In His eternal design He plans what is best for you. Sometimes things go wrong, but God can change your situation so that light radiates from the darkness, and hope is born from despair.

If you feel dejected, think back on all the good things that have happened in your life. Thank the Lord for His blessings and He will bring healing and joy to your life because God is the Giver of all that is good.

We praise and thank You, O Lord, with our hearts, our mouths and our hands, for all the wonders that You have done. Amen.

Start Your Day
by Giving Thanks

I will give thanks to the LORD because of His
righteousness and will sing praise to
the name of the LORD Most High.

Psalm 7:17

A healthy approach and a positive attitude towards life do not come easily to the average person. We are subject to the whims of our emotions. But it is important that we, as children of God, maintain an optimistic attitude toward life.

When you wake up in the morning, your first responsibility is to take positive control of your thoughts and to thank God for the privilege of a new day and for all His blessings.

It requires an act of will to start every day with true thanksgiving, but the benefits are worthwhile.

I want to start my day by thanking You for all the things I so often take for granted – for friends, family, my health and this new day. Amen.

Prayer and Praise

Is any one of you in trouble? He should pray.
Is anyone happy? Let him sing songs of praise.

James 5:13

When a need arises in your life, you may require help or advice from an expert or a friend. It doesn't matter who you approach – you go to that person with the expectation that he or she will be able to help you. Regardless of the outcome, you will be grateful for the assistance given. And you usually express that gratitude with heartfelt thanks.

The same should be true of God. When you bring your problems before Him in prayer and supplication, don't just leave things there. Thank God for the blessed assurance that He cares for you, and that His hand will guide you through all the problems in your life.

I want to praise You because You have promised that You will never leave me nor forsake me. Amen.

Offering Praise

He has sent Me to proclaim the year of the Lord's favor and the day of vengeance of our God, to comfort all who mourn. They will be called oaks of righteousness, a planting of the Lord for the display of His splendor.

Isaiah 61:1-3

Praise and thanksgiving have the power to change lives. When the storm clouds of life obscure the sunshine of God's love; when doubt threatens to destroy our faith in the goodness of God; when life seems to be falling apart – then, more than ever, it is necessary to offer praise and thanksgiving from the depths of our hearts.

You might ask how you can thank and praise God if it seems that there is nothing to thank Him for. Thank God that He is greater than any problem you are facing. As you focus on His greatness, your life will rise above all destructive influences.

O Lord, teach me to rejoice in spite of all the things that happen. Help me to remember that all things work together for my good because I love You. Amen.

October 11

Think and Thank!

I thank my God every time I remember you.

Philippians 1:3

When the path of life becomes steep, and dark clouds threaten to block out all inspiration, pause a while and consider how God has brought you along thus far. Remember all His abundant blessings. At times disaster loomed and you might have felt that everything was lost, but God helped you rise from the ashes of failure.

The key that unlocks the door to a creative life is gratitude. With everything in life, look for something to be grateful for. When you assimilate this truth into your heart, you will approach the future with God-given confidence and the assurance that, in the name of Christ and in His strength, you can triumph over every situation.

Beloved Lord, I recall the blessings of the past and the joys of the present. Thank You for showers of blessings that You pour upon me. Amen.

Gratitude Glorifies God

I will praise you, O LORD, with all my
heart; I will tell of all Your wonders.

Psalm 9:1

Even though religion is a serious matter, some
of God's most dedicated servants have been
lively, happy people. A faith that is void of humor can hardly express the spirit and attitude
of Jesus Christ.

One of the most beautiful things we read
about Jesus is that ordinary people enjoyed
listening to Him and children were at ease in
His presence. This would not have been true
had He been constantly gloomy. He emanated
a deep peace and happiness – joy and quiet
humor enabled Him to love and appreciate
people.

Your sense of humor, enriched by your gratitude and love, is a gift from God.

*I am so grateful for the way in which Jesus revealed
You to us, Father. Thank You for being approachable
and for Your great love. Amen.*

Spontaneous Thanksgiving

Your ways, O God, are holy. What god is so great as our God? You are the God who performs miracles; You display Your power among the peoples.

Psalm 77:13-14

We serve a wonderful God and King! But unfortunately, we often lose sight of His greatness. God is great and Scripture resounds with His invitation for us to share in His greatness.

Jesus promised to dwell in those who love Him and to be revealed through them to the world. When you are aware of God living in you, your attitude to life changes. And as you honestly and sincerely acknowledge the greatness of God in you, your heart will overflow with gratitude for the glory and beauty He imparts to your life daily.

Wondrous God, because You dwell in me through Jesus Christ I can overcome all the negative things in my life and be filled with all the goodness of Your Holy Spirit. Amen.

Singing God's Praise

"Heal me, O LORD, and I will be healed; save me and I will be saved, for You are the one I praise."

Jeremiah 17:14

The person who has not raised his heart and voice to God in grateful praise has missed out on one of the greatest experiences of life. It is sad that so many people consider praise and worship to be something one needs to endure rather than enjoy.

You do not need an organ or the church choir to truly praise and thank God. The simple lifting up of your heart to Him brings you straight into His presence and you cannot help but join with the angels surrounding His throne, singing His praise and glory.

Lord, I want to lift my heart to You and worship You with praise and thanksgiving – for You alone, God, are worthy. Amen.

Be Thankful in Everything

Better a little with the fear of the LORD than great wealth
with turmoil.

Proverbs 15:16

The average Christian is so busy looking for a
spectacular revelation of the miracle-working
God that he is not able to see God at work in
the common, everyday things.

When you have learned to appreciate the
small blessings from God, you will see how
God is at work in your life. The wonder of
friendship, the kindness of strangers, and an
understanding heart are all expressions of the
greatness and the blessings of God.

Make a decision today to never again take
anything for granted. Thank God for His blessings and you will unlock the treasure room
of God and fill your life with new beauty and
riches.

*I praise and thank You, gracious Lord, for the small
things that make each day so delightful. Help me never
again to take daily blessings for granted. Amen.*

Serve God with Gladness!

Worship the LORD with gladness;
come before Him with joyful songs.

Psalm 100:2

I praise and thank You, Father, because You created me and then made me a new creation in Christ. Thank You for the beauty of Creation through which You speak to me and where I can draw close to You in worship.

With gratitude I praise You for Your Word, through which the Holy Spirit reveals Your divine will for my life.

I praise and thank You for abundant blessings – for my family, my friends and all the things that make my life worthwhile. Give me a grateful heart always Lord, so that my life may be a song of thanksgiving to Your glory.

I want to sing to the glory of the Lord as long as I live.
You have done great things and You are worthy
of all praise. Amen.

Rejoice in the Lord!

Then the people of Israel – the priests, the Levites and the rest of the exiles – celebrated the dedication of the house of God with joy.

Ezra 6:16

Many people associate worship with despondency and habit. Through Christ, however, God invites you to receive the fullness of life that He offers each of us.

As you turn to Him you become increasingly aware of His life-giving Spirit at work within you. Seemingly unattainable goals are suddenly within your reach; adversity does not overwhelm you because in Him you find the strength to overcome it; newly found confidence replaces your nervous pessimism.

Day by day your faith grows stronger. Worship should be a joyful experience. Open yourself to the Holy Spirit and He will raise you from despondency to joy in Christ.

O Holy Spirit, come into my life and fill me with the joy of the Lord. Amen.

October 18

Joyous Christianity

"My soul glorifies the Lord and my spirit rejoices in God my Savior."

Luke 1:46-47

Some people think that the Christian faith is a heavy, and sometimes unbearable burden. They frown upon any appearance of light-heartedness in spiritual matters. But God intended something far different.

Christianity does not eliminate joy and happiness from life. On the contrary, it fills your life with abundant joy. Through fellowship with Christ you can know the blessing of His presence every day. The more you praise and thank Him, the more happiness you get from life.

Joy is a fruit of the Holy Spirit. Your faith and surrender to Christ should bring His joy to every area of your life.

Dear Lord Jesus, I continually delight in the knowledge that You are always with me. Amen.

The Secret of a Festive Life

Always giving thanks to God the Father for everything,
in the name of our Lord Jesus Christ.

Ephesians 5:20

If Jesus Christ abides in you through faith, you develop a keener appreciation of the beauty and depth hidden in the lives of others, as well as in the world around you. The greater your gratitude, the more life will reveal its hidden treasures to you.

It is important to be thankful. All through Scripture we hear the resounding echo of the praise of those who loved God and were grateful for His blessings. We appreciate the blessings, but we love God because He is our Father. Our hearts overflow with gratitude for all He does for us.

Thank You, Lord Jesus, for all Your love and gifts that You have granted me. Amen.

October 20

I Will Sing to the Lord

I will sing to the LORD all my life;
I will sing praise to my God as long as I live.

Psalm 104:33

There are many different ways to express your-self in prayer to God when you use Scripture. Allow the Scripture verses to stimulate your prayer life and draw you closer to God. Make them part of your meditations and discover the power of the Almighty God who is able to do all things – the glance of His eye can cause the earth to tremble and set the mountains on fire.

Thus, no matter what enemy confronts you, no matter what mountains block your path, you can be assured that nothing is impossible for our God. Therefore, you can leave your en-emies, burdens and worries in His hands. He will take care of them for you in His mighty power.

Holy God, I delight in Your power and I want to praise and honor You in this song. Amen.

October 21

All the Earth
Bows Down to You

How awesome are Your deeds! So great is Your
power that Your enemies cringe before You. All
the earth bows down to You.

Psalm 66:3-4

The believer need not have any doubt that God
answers prayer! And when He does, we should
sing His praises and thank Him for His faithfulness.

Today's psalm was written after Israel had
won a war under difficult circumstances. The
Israelites wanted to testify to each other, to
the world, and to God Himself, how great and
mighty He is – so that everyone would bow before Him.

To be on God's side is the greatest privilege
on earth. Let us thank God with our whole heart
because we know He hears our prayers and will
always cause us to triumph over our enemies!

*We bow in thankfulness before You God. Thank You
for everything You have done for us! Amen.*

You Give Us Reason to Praise!

We are filled with the good things of Your house, of Your holy temple. You answer us with awesome deeds of righteousness, O God our Savior, the hope of all the ends of the earth and of the farthest seas, who formed the mountains by Your power.

Psalm 65:4-6

God is faithful and eager to answer our prayers and forgive our sins. We need to learn to praise Him with the same enthusiasm we have when we ask for His help. We must also keep the promises we make to God and turn them into deeds of thankfulness.

God is worthy to receive our praise because He answers our prayers and forgives our sins.

Make spending time with God in prayer your greatest joy and tell God how much pleasure it gives you. Burst forth into songs of praise to God and glorify Him today.

Heavenly Father, I will continually sing Your praises because You always fulfill Your promises. Amen.

Spiritual Blessings

Praise be to the God and Father of our Lord Jesus
Christ, who has blessed us in the heavenly realms
with every spiritual blessing in Christ. For He
chose us in Him before the creation of the
world to be holy and blameless in His sight.

Ephesians 1:3-4

We should regularly praise and thank God for
all the spiritual blessings that He gives to us,
such as our salvation and our inheritance in
heaven.

Praise Him also for the spiritual blessings
that you cannot see, such as joy, inner happiness and hope in your heart. Give praise and
worship to our merciful God from whom all
our spiritual blessings come.

When the pressures and troubles of life
are weighing down on you, praise God for
the abundance of His blessings that He
gives you daily.

Merciful and loving Lord, I praise Your holy name for
all the spiritual blessings in my life. Amen.

I Will Proclaim
Your Great Deeds

One generation will commend Your works to another;
they will tell of Your mighty acts. They will speak of the
glorious splendor of Your majesty.

Psalm 145:4-5

God has many traits that make Him worthy of our praise and worship; His majesty; His glory; His mighty acts; His greatness; His goodness and His righteousness; His loving-kindness; His faithful love and His grace and compassion.

For these reasons and many more, we should be full of praise for God. We should tell every generation of God's mighty deeds and acts.

Take a few minutes to consider the glory of God and allow the words of David to lead you in your own song of praise to the Almighty. Then make a point of telling someone else about the wonderful things that God has done for you.

*Holy God, You are surrounded by majestic glory! Help
me to tell others of Your love and grace. Amen.*

My Lips Will Shout for Joy

I will praise You with the harp for Your faithfulness,
O my God; I will sing praise to You with the lyre,
O Holy One of Israel. My lips will shout for
joy when I sing praise to You.

Psalm 71:22-23

The writer of these Scripture verses describes himself as old, saying that his strength has failed. But after he had examined his life thoughtfully and prayerfully, this "old" person was bubbling over with joy. He sings the praises of God and brings to remembrance everything that God has done for him.

Far too often we find ourselves praying hesitant prayers to God and our songs of praise are rather half-hearted. Offer up enthusiastic praise to God and feel the joy of the Lord that will stir inside you.

Lord, my God and Father, I will praise You with thanksgiving and singing and tell others of Your wonderful deeds. Amen.

Pay Tribute to
the Awesome God

You are resplendent with light, more majestic than
mountains rich with game. You alone are to be feared.
Who can stand before You when You are angry?

Psalm 76:4, 7

Anyone who spends time in the mountains develops an admiration for the power of nature. We often feel small and insignificant against the massive rock formations. God created these gigantic structures to confirm His power.

If the whole of Creation trembles before God's awesome power, how much more should we approach Him in prayer with admiration and holy fear! Praise God for His breathtaking power and might. Surrender yourself and your possessions to Him afresh today; give God the honor and the glory He deserves and bring your offerings of time and possessions to Him today.

Awesome Father, in Your glory You are mightier than the majestic mountains. I dedicate myself and all that I have anew to You today. Amen.

Thankfulness
Because Our God Reigns

The twenty-four elders, who were seated on their thrones before God, fell on their faces and worshiped God, saying: "We give thanks to You, Lord God Almighty, the One who is and who was, because You have taken Your great power and have begun to reign."

Revelation 11:16-17

When evil and wickedness go unpunished, we tend to despair of ever finding justice.

The twenty-four elders who sit in the throne room of God praise the Almighty, they thank the One who is and who was because He controls all the events of Earth's history. They praise Him because the earth ensures that justice is served at the right time and in the right place. Do not doubt, because God's justice will ultimately triumph.

In your prayer time today, picture yourself in the throne room of God at the end of the ages, what praise and prayer of thanksgiving will you personally offer to God?

Sovereign God, I thank You that You will ensure righteousness to triumph. Amen.

The Lamb Is Worthy to Receive Our Praise

Then I looked and heard the voice of many angels. In a loud voice they sang: "Worthy is the Lamb!"

Revelation 5:11-12

The Bible encourages Christians to offer prayers of praise and thanksgiving, which reveal their commitment to God.

Yes, our private devotions are very important, but there is an element missing unless we join together with other believers to praise God. We are fulfilling our calling as worshipers when we, God's children, are caught up in worshiping Him.

It is, after all, from worshipers of every place and age that Christ will receive the worship He so richly deserves. May God help us continuously to be found in the company of praying people.

Lord Jesus, blessing and honor, glory and power, belong to You. I pray for the company of other believers so that we can praise Your name together. Amen.

Praise to My Savior

I will praise You, O Lord my God, with all my heart;
I will glorify Your name forever. For great is
Your love toward me; You have delivered me
from the depths of the grave.

Psalm 86:12-13

When we realize the greatness of what God has done for us, we look for ways to express our love for Him. He has been so good and faithful to us. We should remind ourselves when we pray what a magnificent privilege it is to be able to draw close to God in prayer.

We were in the deep mire of sin, but God raised us up so that we could stand in His holy presence. Do not just take this mercy for granted. Today, ask the Lord to teach you to serve Him with your whole heart so that your life will be a song of praise to Him.

*Father, I praise and worship You because You saved
me. Help me to walk in Your ways forever. Amen.*

Why Should We Praise and Glorify God?

Praise, O servants of the LORD, praise the name of the LORD. Let the name of the LORD be praised, both now and forevermore.

Psalm 113:1-2

Why should God be praised and glorified? Why should we tell Him how mighty and wonderful He is? Because He asks us to.

God will never ask us to do anything meaningless or ritualistic. The complexity of the human mind compels it to reach out to something higher and greater than itself. This yearning can be fulfilled by praising and glorifying God. Praise connects us to the One who knows and understands the desires of our hearts.

True praise is one of the greatest inspirational forces in life. It raises you up from your spiritual despondency and brings you into the holy presence of God.

Holy Father, I enter Your gates with adulation, with praise I go into Your temple court. I enter into Your presence with joy and thanksgiving. Amen.

November

God's Grace

The Grace of a
New Beginning

He who was seated on the throne said,
"I am making everything new!"

Revelation 21:5

It is a sign of God's immeasurable grace that no person ever reaches a stage in life where one cannot start over. Each day that dawns is a new beginning. Our God is the God of second chances.

Do not allow whatever may have happened in the past to cause you to lose sight of what the future may hold. If you wish to make a fresh start, make a firm decision to be done with your old life, even though it will still try to enslave you. All new life comes from God alone. Continually affirm that new life flows through you as a result of God's grace, and you will receive the inheritance of new life that is yours in Christ.

Lord of new beginnings, thank You that each new day
Your mercies are new and I can begin again. Amen.

November 1

Eternal Life

For this very reason, Christ died and returned
to life so that He might be the Lord of
both the dead and the living.

Romans 14:9

Many people brood over the unknown. In their uncertainty they fall prey to anxiety and tension.

For the Christian believer there is a glorious truth that emanates from the life, death, and resurrection of Jesus Christ. We know that He is with us right now, leading us through life. He also went to prepare a place for us in God's heavenly kingdom. In this way He assures us that when our earthly life is over, we will be with the Lord forever.

Instead of being consumed with fear and worry, hold on to the promises of Jesus and rejoice in the fact that because Jesus lives, you too will live forever.

*Risen Savior, through faith I know that You live and
that I too will live eternally with You. Amen.*

God Works in Everyday Things

In his heart a man plans his course, but the
LORD determines his steps.

Proverbs 16:9

God often works in miraculous ways. We see
His glory in the changing heavens; we see His
handiwork in the grandeur of Creation.

Yet, God is also the Creator of the small and
everyday things: the perfection of the rose and
the fragility of the forget-me-not. All these reflect a creative God who is also the Master of
order and detail.

We so easily forget that God is interested in
our well-being. Just consider how many times He
has guided you through difficult circumstances.

*Thank You, Almighty God, that You never
cease to work in my life and answer my prayers.
You speak with a thousand tongues; let me
always hear Your voice. Amen.*

You Are a Child
of Royal Blood

You are all sons of God through faith in Christ Jesus, for all of you who were baptized into Christ have clothed yourselves with Christ.

Galatians 3:26-27

You never need to feel spiritually inferior – especially in comparison to other believers. Remember that when God accepted you as His child, He did not do so on the basis of your knowledge, work or worthiness. In His grace He accepted you based entirely on your faith in Jesus Christ and your acceptance of Him as your Redeemer and Savior.

Jesus accepts you for who and what you are. All He asks is that you believe in Him and accept Him as the Lord of your life. Joyfully respond to this invitation and experience the grace and love of your divine Father every day.

Holy God, my heavenly Father, thank You that I can,
through faith, claim the privilege of being
called Your child. Amen.

November 4

Know the Grace of God and Live!

Grace and peace be yours in abundance.

1 Peter 1:2

People are always searching for peace to help them deal with their problems. Do not be tempted to seek man-made solutions, as there is only one true method of handling your life with confidence and assurance – and that is in the power of Jesus Christ.

If you commit yourself and your life to Him unconditionally, then you can rest assured that He will give you the grace required to handle every problem. You will thus be blessed with tranquility and peace far beyond human understanding.

Grace and peace become a reality in your life only through God, so don't drift from Him and forfeit what only He can give.

Loving Master, I thank You, because through Your grace You enable me to face and handle every problem that comes my way. Amen.

November 5

Indescribable Grace

"My grace is sufficient for you, for My power is made perfect in weakness."

2 Corinthians 12:9

When you find yourself in a situation that makes you feel incompetent and inadequate, do not focus on your own abilities. Jesus made it very clear that we are capable of doing nothing without Him, but that with Him we can do anything that needs to be done.

In this truth lies the answer to all your fears, doubts and insecurities. Whatever you do in life, first take it to God in prayer, seek His help and lay all your expectations, fears and concerns before Him. By allowing Him to work through you, you will achieve the kind of success that would otherwise be unattainable in your own strength.

Loving Father, I praise You and thank You for the wonderful assurance that I can do all things through Christ who gives me strength. Amen.

God's Grace Is Sufficient

The days of the blameless are known to the LORD, and
their inheritance will endure forever.

Psalm 37:18

We often hear of people who apparently live virtuous lives and yet are plagued by disaster. Sometimes we want to question God's actions, and it is difficult to agree with Paul when he says, "We know that in all things God works for the good of those who love Him, who have been called according to His purpose" (Rom. 8:28).

However, it is important to remember that God's perspective on life is eternal and He truly desires all things to work for your own good. Paul also says that our present suffering does not outweigh the glory that will be revealed in us (see Rom. 8:18). Take courage and let your heart be peaceful – God's grace is sufficient!

*I thank You, all-knowing God, that Your grace is
always sufficient for me, despite my problems. Amen.*

God's Grace and
Your Problems

*In all your ways acknowledge Him, and He will make
your paths straight.*

Proverbs 3:6

Life can suddenly become filled with problems of all kinds. Regardless of their source, they dominate your life until you find a solution.

If you are experiencing a problem and sincerely seek a solution, direct your thoughts to God and don't focus on the problem. You cannot find a solution to your problem if you do not allow God to assist you.

Allow Him to create order from chaos and to give you the right solution. When God becomes more important than your problem, you will be fueled by a spiritual power because God is occupying His rightful place in your life. You will find solutions to your problems and by His grace you will be able to live victoriously.

Eternal God, I put You first in my life, knowing that You are powerful enough to handle every crisis in my life. Amen.

God Makes Life Good

"Listen to this, Job; stop and consider God's wonders."

Job 37:14

We live in troubled and uncertain times where it is easy to give up and succumb to worldly temptations.

Instead, pause, and reflect on the grace and wonderful deeds of God. Out of the chaos and darkness He created this beautiful earth. He loved us so much that He saved us from the bonds of sin and death. Through the life of Jesus Christ, He gave us an example of the fullness of life.

He promises us eternal and abundant life. Praise Him for all His wonderful deeds, and for His great grace.

Lord, how You fill my heart with gladness. Thank You for Your glorious deeds that I see all around me. Amen.

Grace and Peace in God

I lay down and slept, yet I woke up in safety,
for the LORD was watching over me.

Psalm 3:5 (NLT)

History shows us that those people who walked intimately with God found hidden resources of strength to overcome their setbacks. Those who have an unflinching faith in the living Christ will not waver or break under attacks. Those who put their trust in the all-encompassing love of Christ will not give in to the icy touch of fear.

The same Christ who hushed the wind and stilled the storm at sea when the disciples were panic-stricken, is calling out to you today, "Be strong and courageous; do not be afraid!" Put your trust in Him and experience how His love and grace cause the storms in your life to subside.

*O Lord, I'm so insecure about the future, so uncertain
about what lies ahead. Help me to put my trust
in You day by day. Amen.*

Glory in His Grace

The grace of the Lord Jesus be with God's people. Amen.

Revelation 22:21

The last words of the Bible are this wonderful benediction. How these words soothe our storm-tossed hearts!

We all, at one time or another, suffer from anxiety – either because of a current situation or because we fear the future. In our human weakness and short-sightedness we are not sure how to act. Some people try to handle everything in their own strength, while others throw their hands up in despair.

Remember, the only way out of a problem, and the only reason for success, is the compassionate love and grace of our heavenly Father. The saving and sustaining grace of God permeates our lives. Because He loves you, He blesses you with His grace.

O Lord, I thank You for Your grace. You saved me and redeemed me from death. You are my heart's desire. Amen.

Grace – Rich and Free!

The grace of our Lord Jesus Christ be with you all.

2 Thessalonians 3:18

Where would we be if it were not for the grace of God? The wonderful song *Amazing Grace* tells of a prodigal son who came back to the Father's house. John Newton, the writer of the song, says that he was spiritually blind and lost, but the grace of God touched and healed him. This song reminds us of a redeeming God whose love is so great that He gave us His all through grace.

The Son of God took your guilt and my guilt upon Himself and sacrificed His life to redeem us from sin. His grace extends so far that even when we turn away from Him, Christ waits patiently and lovingly for us to turn back to Him.

Thank You, God, that Your grace has set me free and given me new hope for tomorrow. Amen.

Sufficient Grace

*"You then, my son, be strong in the
grace that is in Christ Jesus."*

2 Timothy 2:1

Many people are not able to work through the problems they face and fear has a devastating effect on them.

Jesus invites those who are tired and heavy-laden to bring their problems to Him and find rest for their souls. He invites you to bring your anxieties to Him because He cares for you. Turn to God in Christ and He will enable you to handle your problems with courage.

Receive your strength and confidence from Him because in all circumstances His grace will be sufficient for you so that you can deal with your problems in a new, assured manner.

*Father, I ask for Your strength to assist me in
times of weakness, help me to know Your grace
that is sufficient for me. Amen.*

Together with God

I can do everything through Him who gives me strength.

Philippians 4:13

When you think of God in all His glory and of yourself as an insignificant speck on the earth, it is incredibly difficult to identify with Him. And yet, the Spirit of God who fills God's entire creation, can also inhabit your spirit. When you realize this, you release a previously untapped power in your life.

When you realize that God, in His grace, has revealed Himself in you through His Spirit, you will learn to draw on His strength, and your life will be vibrant and balanced.

Merciful Lord Jesus, I accept the gift of the Holy Spirit and therefore enjoy intimate communion with You, my Lord and my God. Amen.

For Days When Everything Goes Wrong

"To whom do you belong, and where are you going, and
who owns all these animals in front of you?"

Genesis 32:17

Life must have purpose and significance if you
are to live meaningfully. One of the great truths
of the Christian life is that it changes your attitude. Previously you lived without hope or
expectation, but Christ now plants new hope
in your heart. When you truly start living in
Christ, you begin to look at life with new understanding.

You will never again have to ask, "Is life
worthwhile?" When the thoughts of Christ fill
you and the Holy Spirit's strength saturates
your spirit, you realize the rich quality of your
faith, and your life takes on new and exciting
dimensions.

*Lord Jesus, You came so that we may have life in abun-
dance. Help me to remember to come to You when days
are dark, so that my life may be infused with significance and meaning once again. Amen.*

Enough Grace for You

You then, my son, be strong in the
grace that is in Christ Jesus.

2 Timothy 2:1

Many people try to flee from the reality of their personal crises. Regardless of what your circumstances in life may be, or of how anxious you are about daunting problems, don't run away from them in panic and despair – confront them with Christ at your side. Receive your strength and confidence from Him.

No matter how alarming the problem may seem, you can know for certain that God's strength will be revealed in your weakness.

Under all circumstances His grace will be sufficient for you and you will be able to deal with your problems with confidence.

Father, I ask You for strength to carry the load that is upon me today. Strengthen me so that I can move forward with confidence. Amen.

Praise Be to the Lord

Praise be to the LORD, for He has heard my cry for mercy. The LORD is my strength and my shield; my heart trusts in Him, and I am helped. My heart leaps for joy and I will give thanks to Him in song.

Psalm 28:6-7

When we pray for God's grace we should never forget to sing His praises as well. He is our only hope, our strength and our shield. Even while we are waiting for Him to deliver us from our present dilemmas, we can praise Him for His faithfulness to us in the past. Then our faith and trust in the mercy of God will be strengthened.

God is merciful! How often have we been on the verge of giving up in despair because our situation seemed completely hopeless, and then God stepped in and acted on our behalf?

The might of God works in our favor when we call on Him in faith, and then we can give thanks to Him in song.

I praise You, Lord, because You heard my cry for mercy. Amen.

Our Hope Is in You

Do any of the worthless idols of the nations bring rain?
Do the skies themselves send down showers? No, it is
You, O Lord our God. Therefore our hope is in You, for
You are the one who does all this.

Jeremiah 14:22

God is our only hope in every situation. When
we feel utterly helpless, depend on God and He
will bring you through every trial. If God is our
only hope then we need to be prepared and have
enough faith to wait for the Lord to take action.

If you are suffering as a result of sin, like the
people of Judah in today's Scripture verse, then
confess it. Sin brings only pain and suffering,
but God brings redemption. Confess your sin
to Him and take comfort in the incredible, undeserved grace that God offers.

*Holy God, I confess my sins with deep remorse and
know that You will not cast me away, but will
embrace me with forgiveness. Amen.*

November 18

Experience
God's Faithful Love

You forgave the iniquity of Your people and covered all their sins. You set aside all Your wrath and turned from Your fierce anger. Will you not revive us again, that Your people may rejoice in You?

Psalm 85:2-3, 6

It has become common nowadays to deny sin and its consequences, but there are millions of people who live under the burden of their sin.

A feeling of guilt is often a gift of God's grace to give our lives new meaning, to lead us to a new and more productive life. But an even greater gift from God is His grace that allows us to move in a new direction once our sins have been forgiven.

If we just confess our sin and ask for forgiveness then God is merciful and will forgive us. Think of all that He has already forgiven and give Him praise.

I thank and praise You, Lord, my God, that in Your mercy You have forgiven all my sins and helped me to bear fruit to Your glory. Amen.

God's Great Gift

May the grace of the Lord Jesus Christ, and the love of God, and the fellowship of the Holy Spirit be with you all.

2 Corinthians 13:14

In these materialistic days, it is a real problem for many people to appreciate a precious gift that cannot be valued in monetary terms.

Nevertheless, when you reflect on the sacrifice that God made at Golgotha, the redemption, salvation and hope that He gave us, it should be a source of inspiration and wonder.

There is no way in which we, as humans, could justly repay the Lord for His unfathomable love. Yet, we can open our lives to Him so that through the love of God and the grace of Jesus Christ, the Holy Spirit will enable us to do His work and to spread His love amongst all we come into contact with.

Lord, I always want to glorify You as my Father. Guide me through Your Holy Spirit so that I may be obedient to You in everything I do. Amen.

God's Grace-Filled Love

May the Lord direct your hearts into God's love and
Christ's perseverance.

2 Thessalonians 3:5

We cherish in our hearts the eternal truth that
God's love is free and undeserved. Nothing
that you have done or intend to do can earn
you that. God loves you because God is love,
and this is a great truth for which we are eternally grateful and for which we should glorify
and thank Him.

You are the object of God's love. God Himself lit the flame of love for Him in your heart,
so you must do all you can to ensure that nothing extinguishes this inner flame inside you.

*Truly, You are love! Your Son became man to
demonstrate true love, Father. Help me to
radiate love in return. Amen.*

The Man of Sorrows

He was despised and rejected by men, a Man of sorrows,
and familiar with suffering.

Isaiah 53:3

Christ's suffering was unique and stands out in
world history. It emerges from the plains of time
as a monument of remembrance to the Man
of sorrows' suffering – for you and me. It reminds us that God's grace does not come cheap:
the price was suffering, sorrow and blood; the
blood of His only Son who became human for
our sake.

Jesus, the One without sin, in obedience
to the Father, became sin for our sakes. The
unbearable burden of the sins of all people
through the ages was placed on His shoulders
and He vicariously carried it to Golgotha.

*Lord Jesus, it was for me that You had to endure scorn
and suffering, for me that You had to be crucified.
Thank You, Jesus, that You died for me so that I may
inherit everlasting life. Amen.*

Seek to Please God

For they loved praise from men
more than praise from God.

John 12:43

The only way to achieve the very best in life, and to develop the feeling of self-confidence and fulfillment that is so essential to your peace of mind, is to stay true in all things to your high calling in Jesus.

He is constant – yesterday, today and for all eternity. He will never forsake you or fail you. Place your full trust in Him and not in fallible people. You will never be disappointed.

We do not understand it, Lord, but Your way is always best. You will never forsake us and we know that we are safe in You. Amen.

Remember God's Share in Your Success

By the grace of God I am what I am, and
His grace to me was not without effect.

1 Corinthians 15:10

There are many people who declare that they are "self-made people" and that their success is solely through their own doing.

It is a foolish person indeed who convinces himself that the honor for his accomplishments is his alone. Everyone faces problems and stumbling blocks in their careers. If God's hand of grace was not shielding you, you would never have triumphed over your problems and adversities.

By gratefully acknowledging God in your achievements, and by thanking Him for His grace and goodness, an extra dimension of joy and happiness that you have not yet experienced will be added to your life.

Thank You for blessing us so undeservedly and so abundantly, Lord. You are our salvation and courage for each day. Amen.

When God Lives in You

If anyone acknowledges that Jesus is the Son of God,
God lives in him and he in God.

1 John 4:15

The simple teachings of Jesus Christ have enormous power and if you embrace God, you will have a force in your life like you have never experienced before.

The miraculous truth is that you will not live alone with God, but He will live in you. This is the most amazing and significant experience that you will ever witness; your disposition towards people and circumstances changes; you notice the beauty of life instead of focusing on its dreariness; your objectives are creative and you work positively toward them.

Acknowledging Christ results in such far-reaching consequences that you will stand in wonder each day at what God has achieved in your life through His grace.

I wish to celebrate Your strength. Make me victorious
in battle through Your Spirit. Amen.

November 25

Inconceivable Grace

> "So is My word that goes out from My mouth: It will not return to Me empty, but will accomplish what I desire and achieve the purpose for which I sent it."
>
> Isaiah 55:11

Lord, my God, I glorify and praise Your holy name. Your love knows no boundaries! I thank You that I have meditated on Your promises; may Your precious words become part of my thoughts, life and conduct.

Stand by me through the Holy Spirit so that I will always have a warm heart for others, so that I may perform the true service of love, in Your name and to Your glory. In this way I will not fail to find Your mercy.

Let me never forget how dependent I am on You. I will always hold firmly onto Your hand and so inherit Your kingdom.

Lord, soften my heart to others so I may glorify Your name. I ask for all this through the blood of Jesus, my Savior and Redeemer. Amen.

Now and Then

Now we see but a poor reflection as in a mirror;
then we shall see face to face.

1 Corinthians 13:12

"Now" and "then" are two little words with profound meaning. While we are in this life "now" we have to contend with many situations that look dark and problematic.

But how blessed and happy we will be when we remember both sides of His promise: "now" is a mirror and a poor reflection, but "then" I will see all the glory that God has prepared for His children.

One day we will come face-to-face with our Lord, and only then will we discover how often His love and grace shielded us from disasters and dangers.

I thank You, my Lord, that Your love and grace guide me from day to day. With this blessed assurance I praise and glorify You all my life. Amen.

Provider of Needs

God is able to make all grace abound to you, so that in all things at all times, having all that you need, you will abound in every good work.

2 Corinthians 9:8

God loves the generous giver and blesses him. God Himself gives abundantly so that His children may have enough in all things. He gave His Son, the Holy Spirit, and the excitement of a new, redeemed life. God promises us that we will have all that we need.

If we trust in the Lord completely, we can be certain, regardless of how dark the storm clouds are above us, how great the need – we will always have sufficient strength and grace; we only need to ask God to provide in our need.

From His unfathomable grace, He will every day, in every way, provide in all our needs through life. His love knows no bounds!

Thank You for the quiet assurance, Lord Jesus, that I will always have sufficient strength and grace for every situation in life. Amen.

God Loves You Dearly

"I have loved you," says the LORD. "But you ask,
'How have You loved us?'"

Malachi 1:2

People who have been hurt or broken by life tend to have a problem acknowledging that God is a God of love. You must remember that the love of God is boundless and infinite. It is an unconditional, limitless, eternal love in comparison to our love that is of a passing nature. God's love and care for us is based on that which is good for us, not only now, but in the future as well.

The extent of God's love is so infinite that He is by your side in every situation of life. He waits to support and help you; to console you; to help you overcome stumbling blocks, and to be your Shepherd.

*Thank You, God of love, that I will sit down one
day at the feast of the Lamb, because I love
You and You love me. Amen.*

The Feast of God's Grace

The angel said to her, "Do not be afraid,
Mary, you have found favor with God."

Luke 1:30

God is no respecter of persons – all people are
equal before Him. God has no favorites, but He
is selective.

Through the responsibility placed on her,
Mary revealed the quality of her life and her
devotion to the heavenly Father. As far as it is
known, she led a quiet life somewhere in the
hills of Judea, unknown except to her family.
And yet she was chosen above all women as
God's instrument through which He would reveal Himself to the world.

Your love for and devotion to God may seem
unimportant, but if you offer Him your very
best, He will use you in His own unique way.
Then you will experience the feast of God's
grace.

I praise and thank You, Father, that You reveal Your-
self time and again to me. Use me as an instrument to
spread Your love through the world. Amen.

December

Joy in God

The Joy of Life in Christ

*"Blessed rather are those who hear
the word of God and obey it."*

Luke 11:28

Many people regard the observing of religious principles as a tiresome yet necessary discipline. Christians should have a more positive attitude to their faith because Jesus came so that we could have life in all its abundance. He wants our lives to be filled with purpose, vitality and joy.

The basis of our Christian experience is a relationship with our caring heavenly Father who wants only the best for His children. What more could anyone ask of life? Here you have the promise of the very best that life can offer, and all that God expects of you is to yield to His sovereignty in your life. This is not a lot to ask for when you consider what you are getting in exchange; a life of fulfillment and joy.

*Lord, I rejoice in the knowledge that You redeemed me
and have given me a life of joy and fulfillment. Amen.*

December 1

Jesus, the Source of All True Happiness

To be blessed we must know Jesus as our personal Savior and Redeemer; we must commit our lives to Him and be obedient to His will.

We all search for happiness, on our own terms, and because of this we run the risk of missing Christ's blessing. Man's happiness often depends on chance or luck: a sudden change in our condition. It is something that life offers and then, just as suddenly, rips away.

Man calls it happiness when things go his way for a while, but Christ's happiness is a happiness that is different; it is a joy in Him.

Lord Jesus, I praise Your glorious name for You are the source of all my happiness because You delivered me and made me a child of God. Amen.

December 2

God's Joy

"No one will take away your joy."

John 16:22

The world's joy is temporary and transitory; Christ's joy is a deep well of quiet happiness and, because the source of it is the Lord Himself, it is stable and steadfast.

In the eyes of the world there may be no outward reason for joy, but with Christ's peace that fills our lives and our hearts, we can rest assured that His eternal fountain of inner joy will never run dry and that no one can take it away. Everlasting joy is ours. The Savior Himself promises us that.

Holy Spirit of God, thank You that one of Your gifts is joy. Let me never disappoint my Lord by being a despondent Christian. Amen.

Joyous Assurance!

"Take courage! It is I. Don't be afraid."

Matthew 14:27

Many of God's children have forgotten how to live with joy and peace. They identify with the spirit of the day and forget that, as Christians, they have the ability to rise above the turmoil of our times.

Christian joy is not a giddy emotion that ignores evil or shrugs it off. Christ *commands* His disciples to remain cheerful and courageous. This implies that they should be aware of the worst that can happen and yet, with Christian optimism, hope for the best.

Even when you are afraid and despair stalks you, hold steadfastly to the truth that God is always in control. Christians should be joyful and at peace because they have a living hope in their hearts.

Mighty Redeemer, through Your indwelling Spirit I can face the future with joy and peace of mind. Amen.

December 4

Awake, My Soul!

"Our friend Lazarus has fallen asleep;
but I am going there to wake him up."

John 11:11

How appropriate Jesus' words are for us today! There are many people who need to be woken from their indifference, their hopelessness, and their helplessness. They forget that, in the midst of all the problems in the world today, it is not only important, but also imperative that your whole life should be grounded on your faith in the living Christ.

Just as Jesus raised Lazarus from the dead, so will He raise you from your spiritual stupor and inspire you to live a life of victory, joy and success in His service.

*Lord Jesus, I worship You as the Lord and Savior
of my life, and commit myself anew to living
according to Your ways. Amen.*

Joyous Christianity

My soul glorifies the Lord and my
spirit rejoices in God my Savior.

Luke 1:46-47

The faith of the Christian should be a joyous experience. Your Father takes joy in, and is interested in, your life. He is happy when you are happy and He enjoys your successes as you enjoy them yourself.

Christianity does not eliminate joy and happiness from life. Through your communion with the living Christ, you live in the blessing of His presence every day. The more you praise and thank Him, the more happiness you glean from your spiritual life.

Your surrender and devotion should be such that the joy of the Lord radiates across the entire spectrum of your life.

Dear Lord Jesus, I continually delight in the knowledge that You are always with me. Amen.

Your Salvation Is Here!

The Lord has made proclamation to the ends
of the earth: "Say to the Daughter of Zion,
'See, your Savior comes!' "

Isaiah 62:11

At Christmas we commemorate the coming of
Christ into the world, but we must never forget
about the coming of Christ into our hearts.

If we want to experience the real joy of Christmas, Christ has to pour out His salvation and
peace into our hearts. Thank God that Christ
not only came into the world, but also personally comes into the hearts of those who believe
in Him. He came to find and redeem those who
were lost.

He comes to you today with His hands filled
with grace and forgiveness and blessings; He
comes to turn your sadness into joy.

*Jesus, my Savior and Redeemer, thank You that I can
experience the all-surpassing joy and happiness of one
who has been redeemed. Amen.*

December 7

What More Could
You Want?

Not that we are competent in ourselves to
claim anything for ourselves, but our
competence comes from God.

2 Corinthians 3:5

If you are searching for the deeper meaning and purpose of life, you are on an exciting journey. Fix your eyes beyond the temporal and discover that you are an eternal being created in God's image.

It is only in the light of eternity that your life takes on its full meaning and God's plan for your life can begin to unfold.

God gives purpose to your days and motivation to live life to the full. As you yield to the control of the Holy Spirit, you will become more and more aware of how magnificent life truly is.

Great and mighty God, I honor You. I praise You for revealing Your greatness to me and so enriching my life. Amen.

True Holiness

"My thoughts are not your thoughts, neither are your ways My ways," declares the LORD.

Isaiah 55:8

To many people it seems inconceivable that a life of fullness and great joy can be likened to holiness. Yet true holiness is the most dynamic, creative and meaningful lifestyle in the world.

To be holy implies that you live in a right relationship with God. It causes you to enjoy life to the full and also gives you a greater understanding of people.

The secret of a balanced, joyful, rewarding life is to live in such a way that it is easy for the Lord to reveal Himself through you. This is the way of true sanctification, but is also the road to a successful life according to God's standard.

Teach me, O Holy Spirit, the true meaning of holiness and enable me to live a life that will bring glory and honor to You each day. Amen.

Experience the
Joy of the Lord!

Then the people of Israel – the priests, the Levites
and the rest of the exiles – celebrated the dedication
of the house of God with joy.

Ezra 6:16

Serving God and worshiping Him are not simply duties to perform but actually awesome privileges. Regular attendance of services or places of worship must never be allowed to turn you into a passive spectator. During times of worship, remember that you are in the presence of the most holy God.

Enjoy your life with Christ. Allow Him to become part of your daily life. Then you will discover the fullness of life that He offers you.

Lord, I want my worship to be filled with an awareness of Your holiness. Help me to never lose sight of who You truly are. Amen.

December 10

The Joy of Faith

He who unites himself with the
Lord is one with Him in spirit.

1 Corinthians 6:17

Joy and gladness are not the main goals of the Christian faith, but important by-products of it. The focus and purpose of our faith is the Lord Himself. When His life-giving Spirit fills your heart, the joy of a Christ-filled life becomes yours.

Forgiveness and a Spirit-filled life bring great joy to all who strive to live in Christ. And the culmination of this joy is to live in the constant awareness of the presence of God. You find yourself in fellowship with Him at all times, in all places. The more you become aware of His closeness, the stronger and more meaningful your faith gets. Then joy, unspeakable and full of glory, will flow from you.

Father, I want to express my gratitude to You
for Your closeness by living a life that glorifies
You in every way. Amen.

December 11

Our Calling
to Cheerfulness

Rejoice in the Lord always. I will say it again: Rejoice!

Philippians 4:4

Christians are supposed to rejoice, and if joy fills our lives, we will reap rich rewards spiritually. Many people spread gloom and doom wherever they go, but as a child of God, you can spread joy and inspiration because Christ has given us an indestructible joy that carries us through life.

When you are spiritually sensitive, you have no reason to be despondent. Your daily walk with Jesus Christ, the glorious promises in His Word and God's profound mercy will fill your life with joy, purpose and direction.

Your cheerfulness is not a façade that you put up to impress people but comes from a heart and mind that are in harmony with God through Jesus Christ.

Lord, You fill my days with joy. Your peace flows through me like a quiet stream. Amen.

December 12

Happiness in Christ

He who has clean hands and a pure heart, who does not lift up his soul to an idol or swear by what is false. He will receive blessings from the LORD and vindication from God his Savior.

Psalm 24:4-5

No one can take away the joy and blessings that Christ gives us. We can find joy in Christ even when we are in pain. This joy cannot be erased by sorrow, loss, disappointment, or failure. It is a happiness that sees a rainbow through tears.

The joy that is found in Christ does not depend on our circumstances. It is a deep, everlasting and steadfast joy. It is not something that we can strive for and attain through any human endeavor. It is a gift of God's grace.

The Holy Spirit will strengthen and guide us to obey Christ, so that His happiness and blessing will become our portion.

Loving Master, thank You that the joy You give is steadfast and indestructible – unlike the temporary and transient happiness of the world. Amen.

Christmas: Feast
of the Child

She gave birth to her firstborn, a Son. She wrapped
Him in cloths and placed Him in a manger,
because there was no room for them in the inn.

Luke 2:7

Every Christmas we become children at heart
again. For a short time we leave our mundane
lives and wander down the paths of rich imagi-
nation, of wonder and delightful joy, while we
freely rejoice in the infinite love of God.

Even the staunchest realist finds his heart
stirred when he hears the age-old story of
God's love.

As we experience the mystery of Christmas
both tangibly and intangibly, we are touched
by the wonder of God's love – and our dreams
of peace and joy are rekindled.

*I thank You, Lord Jesus, that I can enjoy the festivi-
ties surrounding Christmas with childlike glee and so
enter into Your kingdom as a little child. Amen.*

Feast for the World!

Do not be afraid. I bring you good news
of great joy that will be for all the people.

Luke 2:10

Today, just as on the night of Jesus' birth more than 2,000 years ago, the angels still bring us a message of "good news of great joy". The presence of the living Christ in your heart will bring you the greatest joy that you could ever know.

The good news of Christmas is that Jesus Christ came to live with you. The angels promised that they had great news for all people – including you. Christ sacrificed Himself for you because of His great love.

Get to know Him as Savior, Redeemer, Lord and Friend. Embrace Christ as the Lord of your life and experience the joy that the angels announced for all people.

Lord Jesus, Your coming into our broken world is steadfast proof that God loves us and cares for us. We praise and thank You for that. Amen.

Can You Truly Celebrate Christmas?

Then they opened their treasures and presented Him
with gifts of gold and of incense and of myrrh.

Matthew 2:11

The Magi understood the true meaning behind Christmas – to give. At Christmas, God gave His best, His most valuable treasure – His Son. And the Child of Bethlehem also gave – He gave Himself in His death on the cross.

Learn the secret of giving from giving. Forget what you did for others and remember what others have done for you. Rather than expecting things from others, ask what you can do for them. Look around you to see where you can sow seeds of joy and kindness and love.

If you are willing to do these things, then you will have brought your offering of gold, frankincense and myrrh to the Lord. And you will experience the true joy of Christmas.

Generous Lord, this Christmas season I once again
offer my life to You to do as You please. Amen.

Take a Break

> "In repentance and rest is your salvation,
> in quietness and trust is your strength,
> but you would have none of it."
>
> Isaiah 30:15

As we withdraw from the confusion of daily life over Christmastime and spend more time in nature, we once again connect with God. Slow down and enjoy the things that we let slip in the everyday rush of the rest of the year: long conversations with family members; the beauty of creation; the delight in a child's eyes; playing with pets; and most of all, digging deep into the Word of God.

Look up into the branches of tall trees, and remember that they grow slowly. Allow God to bring His refreshing strength into your life again, and accept His gifts of peace and joy.

Creator God, thank You for restoring Your peace and joy to me in times of quietness and rest. Amen.

Fulfillment in Christ

As the deer pants for streams of water,
so my soul pants for You, O God.
My soul thirsts for God, for the living God.

Psalm 42:1-2

The same longing that moved the psalmist's heart is evident in the hearts of people today. Although they desire to know God, they wander blindly along paths that do not lead to Him, finding no joy or satisfaction.

However, those who are truly wise know that true satisfaction and fulfillment are to be found only in spiritual things. A proper balance between material and spiritual aspects of life must be maintained; and this is only possible when Christ is at the center of your life.

The Lord cares about every aspect of your life, and when you taste and see that He is good, your life will be rich and fruitful.

Living Savior, in You alone I find fulfillment and satisfaction. Praise Your holy name. Amen.

December 18

Christ-Feast!

> Do not be afraid. I bring you good news of
> great joy that will be for all the people.
>
> Luke 2:10

The world has eliminated Christ from the festivities of Christmas to make room for worldly pleasures. As Christians we need to rectify this travesty.

Christmas must not be allowed to degenerate into cheap tinsel, shining lights and superficial emotions. We must look beneath the trappings and uncover the core of Christmas, letting the Light of the world shine in our lives.

Christians have more reason to celebrate Christmas than others do. The true glory of Christmas is to be found in our hearts – not in the malls or at parties. Let the world see in us the true spirit of Christmas so that they too can come and worship the King.

Holy Spirit of God, this Christmas guide me past the
external trappings to the true inner joy that can only
be found in Christ. Amen.

Festive Season of the Soul

Today in the town of David a Savior has been born to you; He is Christ the Lord.

Luke 2:11

The world is filled with the sounds of Christmas. You can hear festive songs, bells and laughter. And if you listen with your soul, you will hear the angels singing, the joy of anticipation and the sanctified sound of holy silence. You will hear the whisper of the eternal Word that became flesh in Jesus Christ.

Christmas is a continuous season of the soul, and Bethlehem lives forever in your heart. Through God's grace, the eyes and ears of your heart will be opened and you will hear the joyful sounds of celebration because of the Word that came to live among us.

Savior and Friend of sinners, thank You for this season of the soul when we can listen to the soundless Word that became flesh. Amen.

December 20

A Star Shines in Bethlehem

When they saw the star, they were overjoyed.

Matthew 2:10

Christmas brings a feeling of joy, goodwill and peace to our hearts. Jesus came to bring light to this dark world. The light of the star guided people to the manger so that they could joyfully behold their Savior. The Star of Bethlehem still lights your path through the darkness of temptation and wickedness to bring you to the path that leads to God.

During this festive season, and as you approach the new year, fix your eyes upon the Savior of the world. He is your Guiding Star and will lead you to joy, peace and goodwill.

Guiding Star, thank You for leading me along the path that leads to eternal life. Amen.

Christ Is Born!

Jesus was born in Bethlehem in Judea,
during the time of King Herod.

Matthew 2:1

It is an irrefutable historical fact that Jesus was born in Bethlehem. Through this physical birth, God revealed Himself to all of humanity.

In spite of the world's festivities around Christmastime, if you have not experienced the birth of Christ in your heart, you will never know the true joy and peace of Christmas.

If you want to experience true Christmas joy, Christ must be living in your heart and be given the place of honor in your life – the very center of it. When His holiness permeates your life, it becomes a "merry Christmas" in the truest sense of the word.

I thank You, holy Child of Bethlehem, for being born in me so that I can partake of Your Spirit, and so that my entire life can be a celebration in Your honor. Amen.

Worship God with Gladness

Shout for joy to the Lord, all the earth.
Worship the Lord with gladness;
come before Him with joyful songs.

Psalm 100:1-2

During this festive season, let's remember to have heartfelt joy in everything that God has given us and for all that He has done for us. Let our praises to God be like beautiful harmonious music that rises up to Him.

God delights in the joy of His people who are thankful for what He has given them.

Joy, happiness and excitement are often associated with earthly pleasures, but we should learn to associate these feelings with worshiping God and having knowledge of His ways.

As we draw nearer to Christmas, thank God for His goodness, delight yourself in all that He has given you, and share that joy with everybody you come into contact with.

Holy God, I come before You with utterances of holy joy. Help me to share my joy with others. Amen.

Feast of Hope

Always be prepared to give an answer to everyone who asks you to give the reason for the hope that you have.

1 Peter 3:15

With the state of today's world, it would be easy to give up hope, but as the year draws to a close, the blessed Feast of Christ comes to remind us that Jesus came to this world to save sinners.

Regardless of the despondency and despair surrounding us, a beacon of love is shining – the Light of the world – who invites us to leave the darkness behind, put our hope in Him and face the future with expectation and joy.

Advent should remind us time and again that, even if we suffer, Christ is still our hope for the future; as He has been for His children through the ages.

Lord Jesus of Bethlehem, thank You that You came to place hope in our hearts and our lives. Amen.

Feast of Christ!

Today in the town of David a Savior has been born to you; He is Christ the Lord.

Luke 2:11

For all who are tired and burdened, all who are despairing and aggrieved, all who have been hurt and seek revenge, all who are without friends, all who are without real love …

To you a Savior has been born today! He will heal all your wounds in love and grace. He will take away your hatred, pain and sorrow and will console you gently. He is coming to you. He is coming to you now in love and grace, great beyond description. All He asks of you is to embrace Him, love Him and follow Him faithfully. That is the Feast of Christ!

Holy God, we praise and thank You for Your visit to us, Your children, through Jesus Christ. Thank You for Your hope and love, especially today. Amen.

Continue to Praise
and Thank God

The shepherds returned, glorifying and praising God for
all the things they had heard and seen.

Luke 2:20

The festivities are over: the wilted Christmas tree is out the back door, the glossy paper is crumpled, and party hats lie neglected in a corner. The excitement and joy that most people associate with Christmas is now a thing of the past and everybody returns to the routine of daily life.

But this should not be the case! The joyous event that we celebrate on Christ's birthday does not begin and end there. Certainly Christmas is a day of celebration when we attempt to thank God for the gift of His Son, but today and every other day should be reason enough for us to be joyful and praise Christ for His constant presence.

Thank You, Lord Jesus, for yet another Christmas.
May every day of our lives be a feast of Christ. Amen.

December 26

Serve the Lord Joyously

The joy of the Lord is your strength.

Nehemiah 8:10

There are times in our lives, especially when the festivities of the season are winding down, when we feel powerless and grief seems to take hold of our hearts.

Note that our verse today does not state that our joy lies in our own strength. Rather, it says that we have the Lord's joy. What could be better than that?

Our feelings are uncertain and unstable, but the Lord never changes. He is always there, but we must not allow clouds of uncertainty to hide His face. It is a precious assurance for every believer – I serve the Lord joyously and He shelters me.

Please, Lord Jesus, let me serve You with happiness and joy and, in so doing, become a powerful testimony of You in this dismal world. Amen.

Everlasting Joy

"No one will take away your joy."

John 16:22

The world's joy is temporary and transitory, but Christ's joy is a deep well of quiet happiness – stable and steadfast.

In the eyes of the world, it may seem unnatural to have joy in certain situations, but with Christ's peace that fills and encircles our lives, we may rest assured that His eternal fountain of inner joy is guaranteed and no one can take it away.

Therefore I can rejoice because everlasting joy is mine. My Savior promises it. I rest cheerfully in Him because He will see to it that no evil power will rob me of my joy.

Holy Spirit of God, thank You that one of Your gifts is joy. Let me never disappoint my Lord by being a despondent Christian. Amen.

Be Cheerful

Rejoice in the Lord always. I will say it again: Rejoice!

Philippians 4:4

Cheerfulness is a Christian obligation and, if we measure up to it, it brings rich dividends in our spiritual lives. As a child of God, you can experience the joy and inspiration of the living Christ in your life, enabling you to overcome all moodiness when others hassle you, and to rejoice in the spiritual experience that transforms depression into true cheerfulness.

Your daily walk with Jesus Christ, the glorious promises contained in His Word, the experience of God's profound mercy that transcends understanding; these will fill your life with joy, purpose and direction.

*Lord, Your joy is my strength. Even when I suffer,
I know that You will deliver me. Amen.*

Joy in God's Presence

How lovely is Your dwelling place, O Lord
Almighty! My soul yearns, even faints, for the
courts of the Lord. Blessed are those who dwell
in Your house; they are ever praising You.

Psalm 84:1-2, 4

Far too often we envy people because they have
things that we lack. We forget that material
things do not determine our joy and that they
can never give true satisfaction and contentment. Only a healthy relationship with God
can ensure that you will have eternal joy.

Praise God for the blessings that He gives
His faithful children: grace, protection, prosperity, honor and joy. God will not withhold
any good thing from those who are obedient to
Him. He will supply all your needs out of the
riches of His grace. Give Him thanks for His
goodness and bountiful grace.

Lord God, I praise You because You have so generously
loaded me with blessings and all good things. Amen.

December 30

Glorify God

"So is My word that goes out from My mouth: It will not return to Me empty, but will accomplish what I desire and achieve the purpose for which I sent it."

Isaiah 55:11

O Lord, Your love knows no bounds! May Your precious words fill my thoughts and life. Let me always hold firmly onto Your hand.

Thank You for comforting me in mourning so that I can see rainbows through my tears. Thank You for placing a hunger and thirst for righteousness in my soul so that I can live well and do good each day.

Help me to be compassionate towards others so that I can truly serve them in love. Then I will not fail to find Your mercy.

Lord, make me the salt of the earth and a light of the world as I serve You, so that Your name may be glorified in my life. Amen.